Developing
Teaching Expertise

Developing Teaching Expertise

A Guide to Adaptive Professional Learning Design

Ryan Dunn
John Hattie

FOR INFORMATION:

Corwin

A SAGE Company

2455 Teller Road

Thousand Oaks, California 91320

(800) 233-9936

www.corwin.com

SAGE Publications Ltd.

1 Oliver's Yard

55 City Road

London EC1Y 1SP

United Kingdom

SAGE Publications India Pvt. Ltd.

B 1/I 1 Mohan Cooperative Industrial Area

Mathura Road, New Delhi 110 044

India

SAGE Publications Asia-Pacific Pte. Ltd.

18 Cross Street #10-10/11/12

China Square Central

Singapore 048423

President: Mike Soules

Associate Vice President and Editorial Director: Monica Eckman

Senior Acquisitions Editor: Ariel Curry

Content Development Editor: Jessica Vidal

Editorial Assistant: Caroline Timmings

Project Editor: Amy Schroller

Copy Editor: Will DeRooy

Typesetter: C&M Digitals (P) Ltd.

Proofreader: Sally Jaskold

Indexer: Integra

Cover Designer: Gail Buschman

Marketing Manager: Sharon Pendergast

Printed in Canada

ISBN 978-1-5443-6815-3

This book is printed on acid-free paper.

21 22 23 24 25 10 9 8 7 6 5 4 3 2 1

DISCLAIMER: This book may direct you to access third-party content via Web links, QR codes, or other scannable technologies, which are provided for your reference by the author(s). Corwin makes no guarantee that such third-party content will be available for your use and encourages you to review the terms and conditions of such third-party content. Corwin takes no responsibility and assumes no liability for your use of any third-party content, nor does Corwin approve, sponsor, endorse, verify, or certify such third-party content.

Contents

Preface

In a school setting, teacher professional learning is often the mechanism used to build teacher capacity and push for higher levels of student achievement. The underlying premise is that excellence in teaching is the single most powerful in-school influence on achievement (Hattie, 2003), so providing support and resources for teachers to improve their practice should lift levels of student achievement. While this premise is logical, there is still a lack of definitive empirical research on what constitutes effective professional learning for teachers and what impact it has on the students they teach. As Yoon et al. (2007, p. iii) articulated, "The connection seems intuitive. But demonstrating it is difficult."

So, education systems find themselves in a situation where a key tenet of continual improvement of educational outcomes is the deepening of teaching expertise; however, the provision of professional learning is quite variable across contexts. While many systems allocate an enormous amount of resources to professional learning programs for teachers, there is often little evidence that it leads to any real, or lasting, impact.

So, why is this the case? What can we learn from it, and what can we do about it?

In this book we seek to answer these questions. We've been exploring this conundrum because it piqued our curiosity for well over a decade. Our research into teacher professional learning has opened up a world of educational experiences and insights we did not predict. Through our work with schools, groups of schools, and districts that have embarked on sustained professional learning programs, we have gained fascinating insights into the characteristics of teacher professional learning that led effectively to improvement in teaching practice. This research has been a collaborative effort between teachers, researchers, and school leaders from many schools and diverse educational jurisdictions. We are truly grateful for their willingness to trial new ways of working, and we are thankful for their honest feedback on what has worked (and not worked) in their context.

HOW TO USE THIS BOOK

We intend for school leaders to use this book to guide their thinking about how to lead the development of teaching expertise. We're not proposing a lockstep approach; instead, we hope this book can be a tool to aid school leaders as they guide and direct teacher learning within their specific school context. Rather than set a step-by-step process that is required to be implemented in sequence, we encourage leaders to explore the ideas presented in each chapter and deeply consider the key aspects required in their context. Any professional learning initiative for teachers should be underpinned with a carefully considered implementation strategy. Each chapter in this book is aligned to the varied components that schools and districts should consider when undertaking teacher professional learning:

- Chapter 1: What are the key considerations when designing effective teacher professional learning?

- Chapter 2: What does it take to effectively lead teacher learning?

- Chapter 3: Are instructional practices we seek to improve clearly defined? And how would we know if these practices are improving?

- Chapter 4: Why is collaboration important, and how can you cultivate collective expertise?

- Chapter 5: Does our school deliberately and intentionally cultivate a culture of lifelong learning for our teachers?

In this book, we offer practical applications of the research literature to articulate principles and practices that we have seen support the development of teaching expertise. We explore how specific design and leadership approaches can be integrated to form a useful framework for leading teacher professional learning. We account for the increasingly complex educational environments school leaders are experiencing and highlight ways to navigate this uncertainty.

FIGURE 0.1 Book Topic Structure

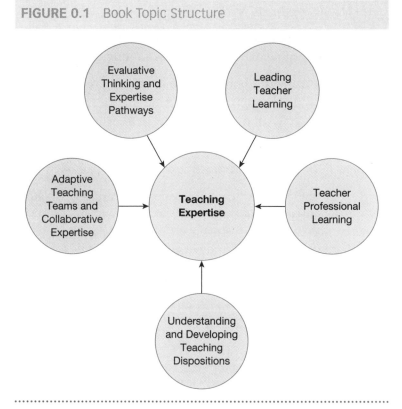

Each chapter discusses a key component of "teaching expertise" based on what our research reveals (see Figure 0.1). Because every school is unique, your starting point will depend on your current needs. We encourage you to apply discretion, as school improvement is complex, and adapting solutions to your context is one of the most important considerations to keep in mind. Before you dig into this book, we encourage you to do the following:

1. Decide which area of student learning you would like to focus your improvement efforts on.

2. Consider the teaching practice that could lead to impact in that area.

3. Read the chapter that most closely aligns with what you believe is a core issue you need to consider to accelerate your improvement work.

4. Carefully review the action items and think through how you might implement them in your unique context.

5. If you are using this book in a group setting, create time and space to walk through the discussion questions together. If not, you may wish to answer the questions on your own.

6. If other chapters seem applicable to the area of improvement in question, read those as well.

7. Repeat these steps for any additional areas of school improvement you wish to tackle.

In each chapter, you will find these elements:

- *Research evidence.* While the book is intended to be a guide for teachers and leaders seeking to enhance teaching expertise, it is important that we establish the evidence base for the approaches discussed. As such, the book will guide you to important literature from within and outside of education that supports this way of working and leading.

- *Principles and practices.* As we explore the research evidence, we will draw it together into important principles and practices that have emerged from the implementation of the ideas advocated in research. The book will often suggest how teachers and leaders can work together to develop evidence of impact, how to enact key practices that accelerate learning, and how to cultivate better ways of thinking and working.

- *Stories from the field.* You will hear from teachers and leaders who have been successfully building teacher expertise and improving their schools. Each story will focus on how a school, network of schools, or school district has implemented the ideas presented in the chapter and what they have learned from these experiences.

- *Action items.* We aim to leave you with clear, practical actions you can test out in your context. While these are not sequential steps that apply to every situation, they are workable, outcomes-oriented activities and exercises to keep you moving toward your goals.

- *Discussion questions.* Each chapter ends with questions that support a collaborative discussion to explore the ideas further. A key element of the discussion questions is to consider what implementing these ideas would mean in your specific educational setting.

Lastly, because we expect readers of this book to possess a variety of experiences and backgrounds, a glossary at the back explains how we use certain industry-specific word sets and concepts. Glossary terms are identified throughout the book in **bold**.

Acknowledgments

This book would not have been possible without the support of and generous contributions from many people. I am very fortunate to have worked with and learned from many amazing educators over my almost twenty years in education.

I am grateful for the collaborators who have supported me to develop, implement, and describe the key ideas we explore in this book. First and foremost, I would like to thank the many school leaders with whom I have worked closely to bring these ideas to life. Your commitment to your teachers and students is truly inspiring. A special mention to school leaders Zoe Smith, Susan Ogden, Nathan Jagoe, and Amelia Eldridge for thoughtfully documenting their experiences in the Stories from the Field. These are valuable contributions that highlight the practical nature of this book.

Thank you to Jessica Sherer and Ariel Curry, who generously read and sharpened the ideas presented in this book. The book is better for it.

I would also like to acknowledge the support of trusted colleagues who continue to support and challenge my understanding of effective teacher professional learning. My informal conversations with Simon Breakspear, Jan van Driel, David Gurr, Jim Watterson, Simon Lindsay, Cath Pearn, and

Bronwyn Ryrie-Jones have all broadened my understanding. I feel very fortunate to have John Hattie as a co-author, and I am indebted to him for his support throughout the writing process. John, your contribution was incredibly pragmatic: balancing critical feedback, encouragement, and perspective to keep the project moving forward. This book would not have come to fruition without your encouragement to pursue ideas.

Finally, I would never have been able to complete this work without the continued and generous support of my family. A special mention must go to my wife, Kate, and my children, Leroy, Darcy, and Mabel. I am truly grateful for your ongoing support and know you sacrificed many things along this journey to allow me to write.

– R. D.

About the Authors

Ryan Dunn, PhD, has almost twenty years' experience as an educational leader, elementary teacher, and researcher. Ryan has advised schools and systems in the United States, Canada, and Australia to develop innovative educational solutions. He has worked extensively in the United States, where he led large-scale research and professional learning initiatives in New York City and California. Ryan is a lecturer at the University of Melbourne, where his teachings focus on teacher professional learning, educational leadership, primary mathematics, and practitioner research.

John Hattie, PhD, is an award-winning education researcher and best-selling author who for nearly thirty years has been examining what works best in student learning and achievement. His research, better known as Visible Learning, is a culmination of decades spent synthesizing more than 1,500 meta-analyses comprising more than 90,000 studies involving over 300 million students around the world. He has presented and keynoted in over 350 international conferences and has received numerous recognitions for his contributions to education. His notable publications include *Visible Learning* (2008), *Visible Learning for Teachers* (2012), *Visible Learning and the Science of How We Learn* (2014), *Visible Learning for Mathematics, Grades K–12* (2017), and, most recently, *10 Mindframes for Visible Learning* (2018).

CHAPTER 1

Teacher Professional Learning

The daily work of teaching is often pictured as someone in the front of a classroom directing and talking at students. Similarly, teaching is often envisaged as an ongoing array of such scenes, lesson-by-lesson, day-by-day, across a school week (Lee & Day, 2016). A fuller picture of teaching – or, more accurately, the work of teachers – should also include the preparation involved in designing the lesson, thinking about and discussing instruction with colleagues, researching practices, testing them in a variety of contexts, and evaluating the impact, to name a few. However, as this is not what most people commonly picture when they think about teaching, the aspects that occur externally to the classroom are sometimes not given the priority they deserve or require. These outside-of-classroom activities can be seen as an "add-on" rather than essential elements of a teacher's normal working day. As such, it is essential that school leaders, systems, and policy makers truly value the time spent not teaching and acknowledge the impact that "behind the scenes" work has on teachers' ability to improve practice throughout their teaching career. The alternative is that professional learning experiences are viewed as an extra, not something that is truly valued or seen as integral to teachers' professional working lives and supportive of their continued development.

> It is essential that school leaders, systems, and policy makers truly value the time spent not teaching and acknowledge the impact that "behind the scenes" work has on teachers' ability to improve practice.

Continuous improvement is discussed at all levels of education, from early-career teachers striving for continuous improvement from their students, to principals and district staff all wanting their schools to evolve and elevate performance. Schools are predicated on a "continuous improvement model." Despite the increased focus on teacher professional learning over the past thirty years, and the expanding knowledge about what constitutes professional learning "best practices," the education community is still grappling with what it takes for systems, districts, and schools to devise ongoing mechanisms for adult learning (Loucks-Horsley et al., 1998; Sparks, 2004). Central to broadening our understanding of effective teacher professional learning is the need for a deeper understanding of the impact professional learning initiatives have on teachers and, in turn, the students they teach.

While extensive resources have been committed to developing effective professional learning, the research illustrates that the very idea of what constitutes "effective professional learning" is contentious, with vigorous debate over what strategies or practices should inform professional learning planning and policy making (Doecke et al., 2008). The debate is often centered on a "top down" versus "bottom up" approach to professional learning. In other words, is it more effective for schools and systems to drive teacher professional learning, or should the teachers have agency over the work? This tension can manifest when the professional learning an individual teacher identifies as most appropriate is not congruent with school- or system-level priorities – for example, a teacher knows from experience she needs to develop her content pedagogy in the teaching of fractions, but the school priority constrains her to focus on metacognition or feedback. To complicate matters further, this all takes place against a backdrop of increasing diversity and complexity that systems and school leadership teams must face. It is no surprise, then, that the very idea of "effective" teacher professional learning can be elusive, even within an industry that has learning at its core.

> The very idea of "effective" teacher professional learning can be elusive, even within an industry that has learning at its core.

The overall process of mobilizing research knowledge into teaching practices is a complex chain of activities, one that requires critique, synthesis, contextual factors, and implementation all working together (Shepherd, 2007). This highlights the increasing duality of the modern teacher as both teacher and learner. It also suggests that 21st century teachers will be unable to navigate the educational workplace without the skills and dispositions that enable them to focus on their own learning needs (Dunn, 2011). This is just as much a leadership challenge as it is a teaching challenge.

School leaders need to carefully consider how they can create an organization that continually supports teachers to develop their individual teaching expertise while ensuring consistency of practice across classrooms. The end result is a realization that catering to individual teachers' needs while balancing the needs of the collective group of teachers is not a simple undertaking.

RESEARCH EVIDENCE

What Do We Know About Expertise?

Studying what expert teachers do is most associated with research by Berliner (1991, 2001, 2004) and his team, who used a range of methods to discriminate between novice teachers and expert teachers, including giving teachers a broad range of scenarios and asking what students might do when students were answering a series of test items. The researchers concluded that expert teachers are more likely to see classrooms as they ideally ought to be – they have a clear model of what a classroom should look and feel like.

Expert teachers are more likely to note atypical events and situations earlier and are able to respond to these in a timely fashion. They are also more critical of their teaching – sometimes deeply critical of their teaching. They continually critically reflect on their practices and consider how they might be able to improve how they teach. They do not rush to solutions (see Hill & Ridley, 2001); instead, they consider and evaluate a variety of viable possibilities, by continuing to ask "What if?" while discarding the not possible from the possible reasonably quickly.

The type of expertise teachers displayed was more aligned to adaptive expertise rather than being routine in their thinking, decision making, and seeing problems as worth exploring to better understand how they could improve their effectiveness in the classroom (Holyoak, 1991). The ability to be sensitive to specific individual learning needs develops as we become more expert. The more we know, the better placed we are to make informed decisions about where to next. The clear implication for this is that novices may tend to benefit from a more directive approach to professional learning as they build their knowledge and understanding, while the sensitivity to their own learning needs allows experts to benefit from a more problem-solving approach (Knight, 2012).

The research on expertise is extensive, yet definite themes continually emerge. For example, it is often overlearned behaviors (e.g., about classroom management, about wait times, about lesson content) that allow experts to devote their intellectual resources to adaptation and seeking out opportunities to maximize their impact on students. It is moving beyond asking students "to do" to engaging them in activities that embrace the challenge of moving from where they are now to where we jointly want them to be. It is moving students beyond participating to striving and driving their learning (Berry, 2020).

Expert teachers have high individual and collective self-efficacy, have high expectations of themselves to impact on all students, and are receptive to feedback about realizing these expectations with their students (Rubie-Davies, 2014). This leads to deliberate, intentional acts of teaching (not sitting back waiting for students to discover knowledge and understanding in their own time), although teachers need to gradually release responsibility to students while they teach them how to become self-regulated and adopt the skills of seeing themselves as teachers. The underlying thinking in all this is what can be termed evaluative thinking – a deliberate valuing of our actions in terms of worth, merit, and significance focused on the centrality of each child (Rickards et al., 2021).

Developing Expertise Through Teacher Professional Learning

Professional learning experiences for teachers have broadened from the more traditional structures, such as workshops, conferences, and seminars, where there was no real sense of follow-up or feedback (Miller, 1995). Currently, teachers are more likely to undertake development activities such as participating in collaborative teacher teams, mentoring, coaching, and observing peers teach. Many of these newer approaches to professional learning take place within the teacher's school, where professional development is focused on the work happening in classrooms. Cochran-Smith and Lytle (1999) supported this shift to embedded professional learning, arguing that the primary purpose of traditional professional-development models was to impart knowledge-*for*-practice. They recommended focus on knowledge-*in*-practice, in which active participation is promoted and learning is embedded in the teacher's normal professional responsibilities.

Educational leaders have the ongoing challenge of adjusting system reforms to the specific contexts of their individual schools. That is, the current educational climate requires professional learning to support reform by enabling teachers to "test their effectiveness and search for new practices wherever they could be found in research and innovation" (Hargreaves & Fullan, 2012, p. 50). In our research and experience, school leaders who design school-based improvement strategies by contextualizing evidence-informed approaches to their own unique context are the ones who create the most significant positive impact for their teachers and students.

> School leaders who design school-based improvement by contextualizing evidence-informed approaches to their own unique context are the ones who create the most significant positive impact for their teachers and students.

There are no simple solutions, just as there is no one single approach or practice that should be implemented without consideration of context. It is clear, however, that professional learning needs to be underpinned by well-thought-out rationales for teachers' learning (Doecke et al., 2008). Servage (2008) found that while studying best practice has merit, it is an incomplete representation of the crucial role of collaboration. Too often, best practice stops with sharing the practice, and it fails to appreciate or learn from the thinking and contextual considerations that went into creating, implementing, and adapting the practice to meet the needs of students. Too often, the focus is on the "practice" (and shared and copied) and not on the evaluative decisions that expert teachers make when implementing this "practice."

Another fundamental tenet of professional learning is that it needs to be transformative (Brookfield, 2003). Unlike learning that targets building skills or knowledge, "transformative learning causes an individual to come to a new understanding of something that causes a fundamental reordering of the paradigmatic assumptions she holds and leads her to live in a fundamentally different way" (Brookfield, 2003, p. 142). This suggests that it is no longer acceptable for teachers to strive to solely acquire knowledge and skills. Professional learning must be more long-term and strategic as we strive to transform the educational system and teaching practices. Transformative experiences force us to confront the possibility that our assumptions may not actually fit. In this way, teachers will voluntarily, albeit sometimes reluctantly, critically evaluate their preconceived notions of what "effective" teaching is. Transformative experiences challenge teachers to think critically about their role and the impact they have on the students they teach.

Added to this, school leaders must acknowledge they do not have complete control over the professional learning process. In fact, for the process to be truly teacher-centered, it might be essential that they do not. Just as student learning is dynamic and requires teachers to be responsive to the learning needs of their students, school leaders will need to embrace adaptive approaches that respond to the needs of their teachers.

Expert teachers think deeply and critically about teaching and learning. Berliner (1991, 2001, 2004) showed that expert teachers are also more critical of their teaching – sometimes deeply so. They continually critically reflect on their practices and consider how they might improve. They do not rush to solutions (see Hill & Ridley, 2001); instead, they consider and evaluate a variety of viable possibilities, by continuing to ask "What if?" while discarding the not possible from the possible reasonably quickly. It is about being adaptive rather than being routine in their thinking, decision making, and seeing problems as worth exploring to better understand how they can improve their effectiveness in the classroom (Holyoak, 1991). Having teaching expertise is also about knowing the limits of your knowledge and being able to seek help and continually learn and collaborate with others to diagnose, problem-solve, and evaluate the impact of the chosen solutions.

> Expertise is . . . knowing the limits of your knowledge and being able to seek help and continually learn and collaborate with others to diagnose, problem-solve, and evaluate the impact of the chosen solutions.

PRINCIPLES AND PRACTICES

The Limitations of "Best Practices"

When discussing teacher professional learning, it can be easy to conclude that teaching – and, more broadly, education – has a reliable research base, so why is it necessary to develop organizational structures for teachers to continue learning? Wouldn't it be more effective to have structures in which everyone is expected to implement the same practices with fidelity? In our experience, implementing research with conformity has definite merit, and there are many cases where this approach can lead to considerable improvement.

Even though there is a strong sense of "what works best" in education (see Education Endowment Foundation, 2020; Hattie, 2009), we need to accept that not every solution works in every context. Indeed, the focus on "Know Thy Impact" is to emphasize the evaluation of impact in the local context – yes, choose high-probability research-based interventions, but the fidelity and quality of implementation on your students by each leader or teacher is what is most critical to understand. In reality, high-probability "best practices" can be delivered with differing levels of understanding, skill, and, therefore, impact. As a result, there is often considerable variability in the results of improvement efforts, even when the intervention is based on research-driven best practices. As such, a core challenge for school leaders is to cultivate ways of working that explore "best practices" as classroom-level interventions that can be delivered with increasing sophistication and expertise.

For instance, breaking practices into more achievable and manageable pieces so that each step can be practised is an important part of expertise development. However, presenting new material in small steps should not be done at the expense of making explicit connections between other important teaching practices. Rather than viewing practices as discrete bodies of knowledge, teachers who connect learning intentions to work on feedback, questioning, or cognitive load theory are far better placed to implement practices with nuance based on the needs of their students.

> Teachers who connect learning intentions to work on feedback, questioning, or cognitive load theory are far better placed to implement practices with nuance based on the needs of their students.

This highlights the notion that best practices are not something teachers simply replicate. Teachers need to be supported in learning to use best practices in increasingly sophisticated ways as they develop their expertise. As school leaders embrace the complexity of "what works best," teachers will most likely gain more than a superficial understanding of the practices they seek to learn more about and implement. If the complexity of the practice is explored in depth, then teachers have the opportunity not only to understand *what* the practice is, but also to understand *why* the practice is important for learning and *how* they can connect it to other evidence-informed approaches.

The Importance of Defining the Purpose

It is evident to anyone who works with schools and systems that schools use a large variety of processes and structures to support teacher professional learning. A quick brainstorm with school leaders will usually result in the rapid generation of a lengthy list of professional learning structures they utilize in their schools: peer coaching, action research, data teams, learning walks, Japanese Lesson Study, professional learning communities, and inquiry cycles, to name a few.

While it is fairly easy to name these professional learning structures, things can become a little murky when we delve into the specific purpose of each structure. In which scenario would you use peer coaching and not learning walks? When would you do the opposite? As a colleague of ours, Simon Breakspear, likes to say, "If [insert professional learning structure] is the solution, what is the problem you are trying to solve?" When the purpose of a professional learning structure is unclear to teachers, or there are multiple interpretations of the purpose, the school can find itself in a position where teachers are working really hard, but there is no observable improvement.

As an illustrative example, let's consider a professional learning structure like peer coaching. Based on the work of Joyce and Showers (1994, 1995), peer coaching has become a widely used structure in many education systems, and schools have allocated significant time and resources for teachers to be able to undertake this process. The evidence base for peer coaching suggests it is a powerful collaborative structure to help teachers develop their teaching expertise. It requires teachers to display vulnerability within their peer-coaching group and be open to exploring practices they are seeking to improve. In essence, it is an act of collaborative problem-solving.

However, if this underlying purpose is not clear, and a culture of collaborative problem-solving is not cultivated, peer coaching can quickly morph into a process in which teachers model aspects of practice they are already adept at. Although observing exemplary practice has merit and should be part of a school's professional learning, it is not the primary purpose of peer coaching. To get the most out of any teacher professional learning within your school, it is important that you match the need with the right structure.

> To get the most out of any teacher professional learning within your school, it is important that you match the need with the right structure.

It is also important to recognize that a school will need a suite of professional learning experiences for teachers to continually improve their practices. One professional learning structure will not be enough to address the diversity of needs within a school, so school leaders need to consider the variety of learning needs among their teachers to determine what structures will be most effective in supporting improvement work.

Professional Learning Structures That Develop Teaching Expertise

One of the key tenets of undertaking teacher professional learning and adaptive ways of working is to try to reach optimal practices as quickly as possible. This can be thought of as a Minimal Viable Practice (MVP). An MVP is achieved by constantly seeking formative feedback on the new practice or approach you are prototyping (Dunn, 2020). Working in this way can expedite the improvement process; results are often realized much sooner, and areas not having the intended impact surface rapidly. Working in short learning cycles with an emphasis on formative feedback loops enables groups of teachers to self-organize and make decisions that are responsive to their context. These adaptive teacher-learning processes might be a fundamentally different way of working than in the past, when school improvement was approached as more lockstep and linear. In a dynamic and complex education environment where a great deal is uncertain, it is strategic – and necessary – to work in short learning cycles.

MVP improvement processes in education grew out of a need for a stronger connection between research, practice, and local contexts, as well as an effort to explore the speed at which improved practices could be implemented. This is the space where adaptive practices began to flourish as a solution for many schools.

STORY FROM THE FIELD

In Australia, the state of Victoria has introduced "Professional Practice Days" where each teacher is entitled to one day per term (four days per academic year) release from their scheduled duties to focus on the improved delivery of high-quality teaching and learning. The work to be undertaken on these days is consistent with departmental and school priorities and selected from the following areas: planning, preparation, assessment of student learning, collaboration, curriculum development, relevant professional development, and peer observation (including feedback and reflection).

The policy is meant to give teachers some autonomy and agency over their professional learning, but it has been challenging for school leaders to cater to the individual learning needs of their teachers while cultivating the collective vision of the school. The following Story From the Field is an example of how one school has found an effective balance.

Developing Teaching Expertise Through Adaptive Improvement Processes at Koo Wee Rup Elementary School

By Nathan Jagoe, principal

▶ At Koo Wee Rup Primary, a small rural elementary school in Victoria, Australia, we collaboratively developed a framework where the goal was to allow teachers to engage in ongoing Cycles of Inquiry to improve their knowledge and practice through newly allocated Professional Practice Days (PPDs). Like many schools, we were grappling with the challenges that emerged around this new initiative, such as the logistics of releasing teachers, coordinating days around other events and priorities, monitoring the learning undertaken on the days, and stretching our substitute teacher pools, to name a few. But the leadership team at Koo Wee Rup Primary School saw the PPDs as an incredible opportunity to bring teachers together four times a year to collectively explore and improve practices in line with specific individual and team needs as well as the whole school's improvement focus.

As a school, we began to formulate an action plan about how PPDs could support teacher professional learning. The guiding action plan was:

> If we work collaboratively to strengthen our teacher practice in alignment with our whole school instructional models, then we will see improved student outcomes.

(Continued)

(Continued)

To instill the moral imperative behind this work, as the principal, I explained to the teaching staff how it linked back to the school's vision statement:

> "We collectively commit to creating an inclusive environment where all students will achieve high levels of learning. We will be relentless in our collaborative efforts to meet all of the needs of our students. We will create a safe, positive and harmonious environment where students feel connected. Students will understand their learning path and be self-directed and motivated learners. We will promote and instill positive values in our students as they become learners with a growth mindset."

The teachers acknowledged the theory of action was a way to enact key ideas from the vision statement. They agreed that the proposed use of PPDs aligned strongly with the school's vision and would provide them with a rich learning experience to further enhance their teaching practice.

Teachers had the opportunity to use their PPDs based on personally identified needs; however, all teachers chose to and still remain committed to working within the collaborative structure.

School leaders were mindful of certain key factors when first establishing and designing the structure of PPDs:

- Teacher voice had to be important in identifying the focus of learning to be undertaken. There had to be genuine agency.

- There had to be absolutely no level of performance or assessment attributed to the learning process. The environment had to be non-judgmental and supportive.

- Teachers had to be empowered to be willing to take risks and build trust. There had to be psychological safety within the teams.

From the outset, all staff and leaders made a collective agreement that all grade-level teams would focus on the teaching of numeracy. The previous year, the school had undergone a significant overhaul of practices in teaching numeracy, and this was an opportune time to further explore and develop teacher practice around this school-wide improvement strategy. Whilst the overarching focus was the teaching of numeracy, each team identified the specific areas to focus upon during the PPDs. Those specific areas of focus were then fleshed out in discussion with the school's head of numeracy, who supported the co-design of the learning that would take place on and in between the PPDs.

Interestingly, no two days ever looked the same for different grade-level teams. Whilst the head of numeracy was responsible for planning some content around the identified focus for each team, the day progressed depending on the particular pieces the team became curious to explore and scrutinize further. It was important this was not predetermined. Grade-level teams always used a reflective model of "what, so what, now what" to ensure they identified specific ways to act in order to improve their practice.

Teams would develop a lesson or sequence of learning around a practice they had interrogated and would undertake a rapid lesson study on the PPD to explore what the learning would look like in a classroom. The team would then reflect and review the outcomes they observed in the classroom and make adjustments to refine the practice accordingly. The lean improvement cycle would sometimes be repeated within one PPD as teams would rapidly iterate a new practice. Teams were deliberately striving to achieve a Minimal Viable Practice they could all utilize in their classrooms. Whilst the design of the day evolved differently for grade-level teams, one consistent through-line with all PPDs was that teachers always walked away having made a collective commitment to explore a new practice in their classrooms. Although there were no formal performance accountability measures placed around these commitments, the school found that it provided a great

(Continued)

platform for conversations to continue beyond what took place on each of the four allocated days. There was a clear enthusiasm that grew out of the rapid improvement process.

The energy around ideas explored on these days ensured there was ongoing dialogue and continued implementation and refinement of the emerging practices beyond each individual PPD. Individual teachers would actively engage with the head of numeracy to plan, observe, and reflect upon their own practice. Teams also continued to review and adjust their practice within their weekly collaborative meetings. Opportunities were also created within whole-staff professional learning meetings for staff to share their discoveries around their teaching practice and extend this learning process beyond their own team.

In the second year of implementation, teams now have an even greater autonomy on the specific focus of their PPDs. With team members changing grade levels and new staff entering the school, the needs of each team evolved, sometimes requiring a new direction. Teams have moved into an area of the curriculum they wish to focus upon and identified the specific part of their practice in which they wish to develop expertise. For example, one team may choose to focus on enabling and extending prompts within their rich tasks in numeracy, whilst another team may choose to explore how to implement strategy groups within reading.

The PPDs have continued to provide teachers with purposeful and genuine learning experiences with their peers that foster ongoing development of their practice. The school believes that PPDs will continue to be such a rich professional learning platform due to the voice and agency that all staff have been given, as well as the open and trusting culture that has been built around these days. For me, as a principal, the key learning about designing a lean improvement process was the immense power of giving agency to staff while also having decision-making structures in place that ensured the practices were evidence-informed and in line with broader school-improvement strategies. I also feel that keeping any sort of formal performance measures out of this professional learning process meant teachers could focus on areas they truly wanted to improve in a trusting, supportive, and non-judgmental environment.

ACTION ITEMS

What Are We Seeking to Achieve?

To decide which professional learning structures need to be in place, we need to carefully consider what we are seeking to achieve; is it improved content knowledge? Teaching expertise development? Collaborative problem-solving? Scaling pockets of exemplary practice that already exist in your school? Teachers, like all professionals, should be supported to continuously grow and learn by developing new knowledge, skills, and capabilities that benefit their students. To ensure a school has the enabling conditions for teachers to continuously grow, at least three key elements need to be supported by the school's professional learning framework:

- An opportunity to develop teaching expertise by exploring new practices in the classroom

- The ability to observe exemplary practice in areas of focus

- A mechanism for gathering evidence of classroom practice to inform future direction

While many different professional learning structures could be utilized to achieve these three key elements of teacher learning, below we highlight three organizational structures that match each of the identified areas. Your school may utilize other structures (Japanese Lesson Study, Teaching Sprints, Cycles of Inquiry), and that is fine – what is important is that you have structures in place to support the key underlying elements identified above.

Peer Coaching: Developing Teaching Expertise by Exploring New Practices in Your Classroom

School improvement asks school leaders and teachers to tackle complex problems in collaborative ways. This way of working calls on the adaptive leadership style, which we unpack in Chapter 2. Support in the classroom using peer coaching is a high-impact collaborative strategy for helping teachers effectively meet the adaptive challenges that school improvement brings to their practice. Peer coaching has a direct bearing on enhanced student learning, enabling teachers to extend their repertoire of teaching skills and to transfer those skills to diverse classroom settings. Peer coaching offers remarkably effective professional learning (Hopkins & Craig, 2015).

Joyce and Showers (2002) focused on identifying what components a professional learning program must have in place for it to impact student achievement. Looking at three potential outcomes of professional learning – knowledge, skill, and transfer – they concluded that transfer is required for the professional learning to truly impact student learning.

Peer coaching is focused on teachers observing each other's practice with the intention of learning from one another. It is a collaborative problem-solving exercise aimed at improving teaching expertise and provides opportunities to discuss challenges and successes with colleagues. The three main action phases involved in peer coaching are as follows (Australian Institute for Teaching and School Leadership, 2017):

Pre-observation meeting:
- Identify the focus of the observation and establish precise specifications of the practice to be observed (this complements the ideas explored in Chapter 4).

- Provide background and give context for the lesson that will be observed.
- Agree on the time and duration of the observation, as well as the time for the debriefing.

Classroom observation:
- The observer records data – what the teacher and students do, say, make, and write.
- Any interaction between the teacher and/or students may occur, if appropriate.

Post-observation debriefing:
- The debriefing occurs as soon as possible after the observation.
- The observer shares data collected relevant to the identified focus.
- The observer and the teacher share reflections highlighting connections between data collected and the teaching and student learning in relation to the teacher's focus.
- The observer may pose questions to prompt further development.
- The observer reflects on observations in relevance to his or her own practice.
- Plan next steps – action to be taken using shared reflections to improve practice, next focus for observations, relevant professional learning required, and so forth.

Learning Walks: Observing Exemplary Practice on Areas of Focus

A challenge that school leaders often face when undertaking practice improvement is how to scale up practices that already exist within the school – that is, how to support these practices to be more widespread. As we discuss briefly in Chapter 3, learning walks are an organization process that gives teachers the opportunity to observe what specific practices are taking place in a range of classrooms. The premise of a learning walk is for the walkers to have the opportunity to observe exemplary practice in action and to watch the impact of the exemplary practice on students. The intention is for them to observe and then explore the thinking and contextual considerations that went into creating, implementing, and adapting the practice to meet the needs of the students.

As a school begins to seek practical and context-specific interventions informed by current research, some teachers, for a range of reasons, may be able to enact these practices effectively within their classrooms earlier than other teachers. In this instance, it is important to have built-in mechanisms for teachers to be able to share these emerging positive practices.

A learning walk encourages improvement through open, transparent sharing of practice. It is focused on the needs of the walkers, and it offers them an opportunity to observe other practices occurring in the school with the intention of trialing these within their own classrooms. A learning walk usually follows a four-step process:

1. A pre-walk meeting, in which a clear focus and observation protocols are established

2. Observation of practice in multiple classrooms related to the agreed focus (ten to fifteen minutes)

3. A short debriefing after each classroom visit, in which the group engages in reflective, non-judgmental dialogue about what was observed, questions, and implications

4. A final debriefing, in which the evidence collected is reviewed, insights from individual classroom debriefings are linked, questions raised are examined, and next steps for the walkers to undertake in their classrooms are co-designed

DEVELOPING TEACHING EXPERTISE

Instructional Rounds: Gathering Evidence of Classroom Practice to Inform Future Direction

Since instructional rounds were introduced into education over a decade ago, there have been many variations and adaptations of this organizational improvement process. Instructional rounds were inspired by the medical-rounds model used by physicians to observe, discuss, and analyze practice. They were "intended to help education leaders and practitioners develop a shared understanding of what high-quality instruction looks like and what schools and districts need to do to support it" (City et al., 2009).

Instructional rounds are an effective process for gathering observational evidence from a range of classrooms to develop patterns aligned to key improvement initiatives. They are a way of collectively gathering data, undertaking analysis, and generating next steps specific to practice-improvement work.

Instructional rounds can be undertaken at any time during the academic year, and it is recommended that they be repeated frequently to establish evidence of impact – to gather a snapshot of practice from a range of classrooms to establish the level and quality of implementation. The idea of observing instruction and calibrating interpretation of observational data is a way to both ensure inter-rater reliability among observers and create shared understanding of current practices and develop future direction. Feedback is not given to individual teachers, as the aim is to establish school patterns. Key actions involved are the following:

- Establish a team (leaders and teachers), and agree on the scope and key areas to be observed. Be as specific as possible in this step, to define the parameters and to keep evidence collection focused.

- Observation groups collect evidence related to the identified focus and observation protocol. The instructional round team visits a range of classrooms for up to twenty minutes to gather evidence. The observations should be low-inference and descriptive, recording only what is seen and heard, without any positive or negative inferences.

- After the observation, the group uses the agreed-upon observation protocol as a basis for discussion. It is important the discussion remain within the original parameters agreed upon at the beginning of the process. The group seeks to unearth patterns of practice emerging in the school.

- The group considers next steps and establishes recommendations for the next iteration of improvement work. Recommendations should be specific and can be time-bound; what will we do next week, next month, or even next year?

DISCUSSION QUESTIONS

- How well do we currently balance individual teachers' learning needs and whole-school direction?

- Do we have a well-defined suite of professional learning experiences? And is the purpose of each structure matched to the learning we are seeking?

- Do we have mechanisms in our school to establish the varying levels of teaching expertise that exist? Are these mechanisms non-judgmental and about support, growth, and continual learning? Or are they more linked to evaluation and accountability?

- What would it take to develop a suite of professional learning experiences that support effective teacher professional learning?

CHAPTER 2

Leading Teacher Learning

Over the last ten years, researchers in the field of teacher professional learning have realized that passively disseminating research – "packaging and posting" – is unlikely to have a significant impact on people's behaviors (Nutley et al., 2007). Like so many aspects of working in schools, the application of research is emerging as a largely social process, with personal interactions and relationships being key factors in determining how evidence gets used and applied in practical settings. Having the opportunity to discuss research helps practitioners gain a deeper understanding and sense of ownership of the findings and, in doing so, enables them to integrate evidence more relevantly and sensitively in professional settings (Cooper, 2010).

In this respect, it is unsurprising that collaborative approaches that support direct engagement and dialogue between researchers and practitioners are proving to be particularly effective (Nutley et al., 2007). As such, our notion of knowledge mobilization in education requires extending beyond just communicating research to looking at how it is effectively engaged with and applied to practice. A key principle is to move beyond the pursuit of novel and new practices and instead focus intently on improving student learning.

> A key principle is to move beyond the pursuit of novel and new practices and instead focus intently on improving student learning.

As Robinson (2017) highlighted, not all change leads to improvement. Because of this, the difficult part is not the decision to pursue evidence-informed practices; the complexity is in the implementation and mobilization of research evidence. With school-level implementation of evidence-informed practices, there is no predetermined recipe for success that can be replicated to ensure success. What might have been successful in one school may miss the mark in another. While the evidence base may be solid, the fact remains that learners are different with respect to their prior knowledge, beliefs, needs, and/or motivations to participate, and this can change everything (Kirschner & Surma, 2020).

RESEARCH EVIDENCE

Globally, teachers are accountable for growing expectations around progress in student learning. In the Australian context, schools are being asked to ensure growth in skills, knowledge, and capabilities (Australian Curriculum, Assessment and Reporting Authority, 2014) for an increasingly diverse group of learners; analyze and adopt data-driven practices; and gather evidence of student progress in learning. These intersecting pressures are creating substantial challenges for teachers, who are often only provided with one-off workshops highlighting "best practices," which in many cases add to the complexity of their work rather than support the development of their expertise.

There is increasing agreement that there are no ready-made instructional solutions that can simply be replicated to cater to unique classroom and school contexts. There will always need to be consideration of current levels of expertise and sensitivity to the pre-existing practices within a school. This creates often-overlooked complexities in school-improvement work, with the potential for unanticipated responses and consequences (Axelrod & Cohen, 2000; Miller & Page, 2007). As evidenced by Dunn et al. (2019), an approach that enables groups of teachers to collaboratively design, implement, and evaluate practices has clear benefits for teachers and their students.

While the growing educational research evidence base can support the design of frameworks and interventions based on pedagogic best practices (e.g., Evidence for Learning, 2017; Hattie, 2009), the core challenge is to ensure best practices can be delivered with increasing levels of expertise and, therefore, impact. As such, leaders should approach teacher professional learning with a commitment to continually developing teachers' expertise.

If leaders embrace and explore the complexity of best practices, then the approach will most likely end with teachers gaining more than a superficial understanding of those practices. In other words, teachers will have the opportunity not only to understand *what* the practice is, but also to understand *why* the practice is important for student learning. The best way for teachers to learn these practices is over plenty of time, with support, and with clear impact measures and meta-cognitive processes built in so that the subtlety, nuance, and connections to other practices can be understood and leveraged. Teacher professional learning that cultivates this mindset is more likely to develop the sophisticated teacher practices that will cater to the diverse contexts and classrooms inherent in every school system.

In the complex and rapidly changing world we live in, the ability to constantly adapt and respond to varied contexts is more critical than ever. School leadership is more akin to improvised art forms than many would imagine. As Heifetz et al. (2009) articulated:

> Everything you do in leading adaptive change is an experiment. Many people, however, choose not to see it that way, feeling and succumbing to the enormous pressure to produce certain results from their actions. Framing everything as an experiment offers you more running room to try new strategies, to ask questions, to discover what's essential, what's expendable, and what innovation can work. (p. 277)

Heifetz et al. highlight that although an implementation strategy is evidence of your commitment to improvement, it is not necessarily the solution on how to get from one point to another. The experimental mindset involves testing a hypothesis, looking for contrary data, and making course corrections as you generate new knowledge. Adaptive practices are best suited to complex environments, such as educational settings, where there is a need to test and discover. Ideas and solutions may have been formulated in advance, yet a great deal of learning, reflection, and understanding is still required. In this instance, forming a detailed linear plan will make only limited sense, because we know things will most likely turn out differently when we begin learning from early implementation. A clear goal is still necessary, and a pathway to improvement should still be developed (see expertise pathways in Chapter 3); however, there is a clear understanding that learning and adapting within this place will be integral to success.

Think of a sailing ship heading north using Polaris, the North Star, to guide its journey. The ship's captain has a clear direction in mind but may veer in other directions as needed to catch the wind that will most effectively move the ship in the proposed northerly direction. The destination is clear, but a linear pathway is not the most effective to take. An adaptive mindset understands that taking the first step is important, because once we take that first step, we then discover the most appropriate second step. Research has illustrated that adaptive practices, in which school-based solutions are collaboratively designed, implemented, and evaluated, have definite benefits for teaching practice (Dunn et al., 2019).

Ultimately, school-improvement work is an ongoing journey, and each school is unique, so there is never going to be an improvement path that is so constraining that adjustments are not required as the improvement journey unfolds. To advocate for this would be an oversimplification of the complexity within which schools work. With that said, we have developed and tested the ideas put forward in this chapter in a diverse range of schools in different systems and countries. They are evidence-driven interventions, designed to be customizable to your specific education context.

Heifetz and Laurie (1997) popularized the idea of two distinct types of improvement efforts in any organization: technical problems and adaptive challenges. A technical problem is one that can be solved with existing knowledge and skills. Solutions to technical problems are achieved by implementing routines and standard operating procedures with rigor and fidelity.

A school-based example of a technical problem is the procedure used for a fire drill. School leaders identify fire-drill procedure as an area in which they need to be more efficient; they develop a solution, implement it well, then monitor and report on the process. The key aspect is rigid adherence to a predetermined (and possibly co-designed) process or procedure. A directive leadership approach is often the most efficient and effective way to solve technical problems.

Adaptive challenges require moving beyond what you – at a school-wide or an individual level – currently know, understand, and do. Although you might be able to hypothesize a possible solution, you will still need to test and learn through iterative cycles to establish a workable context-specific solution (see Figure 2.1). By definition, adaptive challenges do not lend themselves to obvious solutions, and school leaders need an organizational strategy for dealing with the complexity that adaptive challenges surface.

FIGURE 2.1 Technical Problems vs. Adaptive Challenges

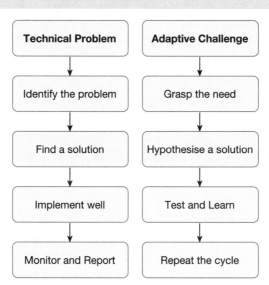

The COVID-19 pandemic is a recent example of a global adaptive challenge for governments, businesses, communities, and schools. This incredibly complex problem meant we could not rely on implementing a previously identified solution or response. The problem of how to influence complex situations toward favorable outcomes, and away from unfavorable ones, was arguably at the core of the important and difficult challenges we faced. As nations across the world rapidly attempted to design solutions based on emerging information and needs, they often approached it as an iterative testing and learning cycle. As new evidence emerged, leaders hypothesized solutions, implemented strategies, and sought evidence of implementation and impact. Next steps were then determined, based on early impact evidence. This cycle enabled a rapid response but also created an environment in which we knew things could change based on new data. Adaptive leadership practices were best suited to respond to this significant challenge.

As schools embark on their improvement journey, they will no doubt encounter both technical problems and adaptive challenges. Interestingly, early improvement efforts may see school leaders make significant gains by using a directive approach and addressing technical problems by creating consistent planning templates, developing and implementing a school-wide instructional model, and establishing clear learning protocols. However, often these efforts reach an expertise ceiling: there may be consistency in the initial implementation, in which the teachers are all working in the same way, but evolving into the next level of work might not be clear. This can occur when there is rigid adherence to rules and procedures, rather than a view of the school as a dynamic organization seeking to continually respond to students' needs and changing contextual factors. As a result, consistency can mean performance begins to plateau. Mourshed et al. (2010) discussed this phenomenon at a system level and noted that while leaders might observe early gains through a more directive and technical approach, these usually do not sustain over the long term. So, while the need to implement something like a new reporting system might be best approached as a technical problem through a directive leadership lens, other problems should be approached through an adaptive lens.

However, as Heifetz and Laurie (1997) highlighted, working adaptively is not a silver bullet for education. It is definitely not the solution to all challenges that arise in schools. Adaptive ways of working are best suited to situations in which there is significant uncertainty and considerable elements of the improvement initiative are still to be discovered. In essence, working adaptively is ideal for *complex* situations in which you have a strong sense that a linear pathway is not likely to occur. If there seems to be uncertainty around what might work and how it might be implemented, the level and degree of uncertainty can give clues as to how adaptive approaches could be effective. Embracing the concept of complex adaptive systems provides a valuable toolkit for understanding and addressing a broad range of educational issues. Chapter 4 explores how to cultivate adaptive ways of thinking and working within a team setting.

PRINCIPLES AND PRACTICES

The Role of School Leaders in Teacher Professional Learning

School leaders make a very real difference to student learning and achievement. But because their influence is usually indirect, it has often been difficult to link their actions directly to student outcomes (Hopkins et al., 2011). Fortunately, recent research has explored the connection between leadership and learning.

The role of an effective school leader is one of many diverse stances. An effective leader is aware of different leadership practices and knows when and how to apply them depending on the situation. Everything is undertaken with the purpose of helping teachers understand and apply improved instructional practices.

To effectively lead teacher professional learning, school leaders need to employ adaptive approaches that enable them to respond, adjust, and refine their work based on emerging evidence from their improvement efforts. School leaders need to consider how to give teachers the opportunity to deliberately and intentionally embed new practices over time, so that subtlety, nuance, and connections to other evidence-informed instructional practices are not only understood, but also leveraged. We have found that creating the structures, skills, and dispositions required to engage in rapid-cycle improvement is a key lever for both immediate and sustained success.

Leading an organization to become more adaptive in the way it approaches teacher learning requires developing specific leadership skills, attitudes, and collaborative structures that enable and foster adaptive performance. In other words, school leaders need to develop an adaptive stance; they should be constantly looking for ways to test their knowledge about the teaching and learning within their unique school context.

An adaptive stance is both an intellectual stance that creates the preconditions for being adaptive and a particular pattern of decision-making in complex situations (Grisogono & Radenovic, 2007). Operational adaptability is essential to developing situational understanding and to the ability to work through complex situations as they arise. Although it is impossible to anticipate the precise dynamics of the future, cultivating adaptive leadership should enable schools to react quickly to rapidly changing conditions and seize upon unforeseen opportunities.

Cultivating Adaptive Ways of Working and Thinking

As a response to a rapidly changing and complex world, many organizations are actively exploring methods in which they can become more adaptive and nimble in their approach. While they might be drawing on similar guiding principles and approaches, there is no one way this looks in practice. "Adaptive" is both a framework and a capability that includes a set of principles and practices. In our work over the past decade with school leaders who have sought to utilize adaptive ways of working, some key tenets to consider have become apparent:

- *Develop a mindset of acceptance.* We need to accept the complexity of the environment we are working within. As a leader, you need to accept ambiguity and uncertainty; by doing this, you can begin to understand that nothing remains static and we are constantly evolving. This mindset will help you deal with the unexpected, because you will accept the unexpected as a normal part of working within complexity.

- *Empower teachers to respond to their unique context.* Adaptive leaders continually search for impediments that may be hindering the growth of their teaching teams and endeavor to solve these. They support teaching teams to make rapid progress by helping them self-organize and make decisions that are responsive to their context and based on best evidence. They do not leave responsibility entirely with teachers and are still part of the decision-making process, but they view one of their primary roles as supporting teachers to be able to do the work they need to do. They exhibit practices such as deep listening, self-awareness, and commitment to others.

- *Develop the situation through action.* When exploring adaptive challenges, effective leaders understand that solutions are being developed from an incomplete evidence base. Complex situations entail inevitable uncertainty. As such, school leaders should be prepared to develop the situation through action. An adaptive mindset understands that taking the first step is important, because in taking that first step, we discover what the most appropriate second step might be.

- *Focus on teams, not individuals.* Studies by the MIT Center for Collective Intelligence (http://cci.mit.edu) illustrate that although the intelligence of individuals affects team performance, the team's collective intelligence is more important. These studies also suggest it is easier to change team behaviors than individual behaviors as a driver for improvement.

- *Design lean improvement processes.* Lean improvement processes are achieved by attempting to come up with the leanest solution that might lead to improvement. By keeping the process as lean as possible, the aim is to prototype a practice by minimizing the required resources, to rapidly discover whether the proposed practices are proving to be effective in your unique context. Consider the approach that educational systems took when moving to remote teaching as a response to COVID-19. Practices were rapidly trialed; the efficacy of these practices was quickly established; and practices were continued, refined, or put on hold as further investigation took place.

- *Foster psychological safety.* Psychological safety refers to an individual's perception of the consequences of taking an interpersonal risk or to his or her belief that he or she will not be seen as ignorant, incompetent, negative, or disruptive for choosing to take risks. In a team with high psychological safety, teammates feel safe to take risks around their team members. They feel confident that no one on the team will embarrass or punish anyone else for admitting a mistake, asking a question, or offering a new idea (Edmondson, 2012). This is expressed through specific behaviors, such as encouraging teachers to express opinions and ideas, promoting collaborative decision-making, supporting information sharing and teamwork, and being non-judgmental (Chen et al., 2011). Some specific actions to foster psychological safety can be found in the Action Items in Chapter 5.

STORY FROM THE FIELD

Two key principles for cultivating collaborative expertise are to ensure that the group has agency over the process and to ensure the transparency of decision-making processes. It is important not to fall into cumulative conversations in which everyone simply agrees with one another, causing the group to explore and then implement suboptimal strategies. At this point, the team should engage in exploratory conversations and critical investigation of ideas. This relies on the group members analyzing, critiquing, and challenging the ideas and practices they are considering. Since this is easier said than done, how can a leader support teacher teams to work in such a way? The work of school leaders at Graceville State School provides key insights.

Graceville State School, an elementary school located in the southern part of Brisbane, Australia, opened in 1928 and since that time has been providing high-quality educational experiences aligned to the school motto, "Strive to Excel." Recently, principal Zoe Smith has led it through significant improvement work on evidence-informed practices, by carefully designing experiences that cultivate a shared vision. She is a thoughtful educational leader who cares deeply about improvement initiatives that are developed and co-owned by her school community. Below, she describes her experience in developing community agency and collaborative decision-making as a foundation for meaningful teacher inquiry.

Developing Group Agency and Collaborative Decision-Making at Graceville State School

By Zoe Smith, principal

ESTABLISHING STRONG FOUNDATIONS FOR TEACHER INQUIRY

Two years ago, we embarked on a journey to develop a school-wide approach to the teaching and learning of writing that would meet the needs of our school community. From the outset, we understood this to be an adaptive challenge where we would need to engage in cycles of rapid inquiry to develop a context-specific solution. To begin this process, we sought a small group of committed educators who were curious to learn and connect as a community of inquirers, with the intent of trialing new writing practices that would form the basis for a school-wide approach to writing. The team that was established was a vertical team of fifteen educators across our elementary school community.

The team began by discussing and establishing a common purpose and group norms to underpin their collaborative inquiry. The team discussed the importance of establishing a shared direction in this work and developed explicit norms about how they would communicate, review evidence, implement ideas, challenge each other, and make collaborative decisions. The team developed the following terms of reference for their collective work:

> As an open-minded writing team, we will collaboratively research, consult and challenge to reach democratic decisions that will inspire passionate and influential student authors. As a group, we will advocate for the decisions made and support implementation within the school community.

With this in mind, they began to work together to design the inquiry approach they would use to frame their learning journey. Positioning themselves as inquirers, they understood they could only plan so far ahead and had to be comfortable living with uncertainty, knowing that through the testing and learning implementation cycles they needed to keep the big picture of where they were going in mind; responding to what was revealed to them through their learning would inform and guide the essential next step to take. This was a key learning: implementation is not a linear process, and we need to respond to early implementation.

(Continued)

(Continued)

As a school leader, I was aware how critical the step would be to ensure that teachers were comfortable working within this ambiguous space when exploring writing practices. It became clear this step required strong support and reassurance from school leadership to ensure that the teachers genuinely explored new practices rather than exploring things that might have been safe but not necessarily led to improved writing practices among students. We wanted teachers to embark on a journey to genuinely stretch their expertise and trial new evidence-informed writing practices to determine their efficacy in our context, not report on the status quo.

WHAT WE DID

After co-designing the approach the team would undertake to explore a range of practices in writing, the team began to formulate a set of understandings and goals as a way to stay focused on what they were specifically trying to achieve. After the diverse perspectives of the team were explored, this was distilled into a guiding question to drive the collaborative inquiry: "What makes an effective author?"

The first part of the inquiry cycle saw the team *tuning in to* the *current reality* of the school and the broader educational environment in relation to writing. The team broke into groups to explore current understandings of what made an effective author, being sure to seek and gather evidence from a wide range of sources, including known federal and state documents, teachers' professional knowledge, parents' practical local knowledge and experiences, and student focus groups.

The team organized a series of real-life experiences with known authors for students, teachers, and parents/carers within the school community, the outcome of which was quite profound and resulted in a rich array of feedback that was included as an equally important piece of evidence for the team to consider. The team made the decision to share the findings of the first phase of their inquiry with the school community. To the team's delight, the interest was overwhelming.

The impact of the Author provocation had "lit a fire" inside the majority of the school community, and interest in the inquiry into writing grew even more once all members of the school community could see how their thinking and voice had been included as part of the process. Agency and empowerment emerged as a key theme to building a movement behind the work. The team could see that if they continued to keep the wider community included and informed, it was likely there would be continued engagement and ownership.

In relation to the teaching staff, the sharing session excited teachers to engage and put forward ideas of known approaches that could support the aspirations the community consultation had identified. Teachers who were not on the writing team were also eager to explore different evidence-informed approaches to the teaching of writing and experiment with them in their classrooms. This led to thirteen unique approaches to writing put forward for the team to consider. The next step in the collaborative inquiry had been clearly revealed: What mixture of approaches would best suit our unique context?

As the team entered the "finding out" phase of the inquiry, they realized they could not deeply analyze and implement all thirteen proposed approaches to see which one worked best. So, they broke into smaller teams and undertook a mixture of researching the evidence base for the approaches, visiting schools that were implementing the approach for insights, and testing promising approaches within their own classrooms. After ten weeks, the team reconvened to share and sort out their learnings and identify any questions they still had.

To support the evaluation, the team created a matrix of evidence aligned with the identified key goals and understandings. This

(Continued)

(Continued)

matrix was a useful visual tool for determining the approaches
that would be best able to meet the needs identified by our
school community. As the team started to discuss and justify
the relevance of each approach, different team members began
to form a hierarchy of importance related to the different goals.
We wondered what this was telling us. Were our beliefs and
assumptions about the teaching and learning of writing now being
revealed? At this point, the team decided to share the findings
with the wider teaching staff and ask them to apply the matrix.
The team was curious to see whether the rest of the staff would
have a similar reaction. Once again, a range of beliefs started
to emerge. It became quite clear we needed to inquire into
underpinning beliefs about the teaching and learning of writing in
order for us to move forward as a teaching group.

The tangible outcomes were far from what the team had anticipated
at the beginning of the inquiry; however, the process was more
powerful and deeply owned by the school community. The team's
action to move the school forward was not any one program or
approach but a guiding set of agreed-upon beliefs, with statements
of what the beliefs would look like when enacted in the classroom.
Underpinning the document were a range of best practices the
team had identified from their research that aligned with the beliefs.
The next critical step was to support the teachers in revising their
own practices to align with the newly established guiding beliefs.
The school moved to an adaptive growth model, which puts both
teacher and student learning at the heart of what we do.

KEY LEARNINGS AND RESULTS

As inquirers, when we started on the journey, we knew it could be
a long one with many twists and turns. We were surprised at the
final outcome, however, and believe the action taken to be the best
outcome for all members of the school community. As a school,
we will continue to use reflective inquiry processes to debrief our

progress and affirm or adapt as necessary. The purpose of our inquiry was to make a difference in outcomes and experiences that matter for our learners. As evidenced through this Story From the Field, the writing team's inquiry fostered curiosity, engagement, and community ownership among writers at all levels across our school. As a result, we have seen students achieve higher levels of sophistication in their writing on both school-based and standardized assessments. Our teachers remain professionally curious about our writing practices, and they continue to engage with and learn through our adaptive process; we anticipate continued improvement in student learning as a result.

ACTION ITEMS

While working with school leaders, we discovered that in addition to a focus on developing adaptive practices, effective leaders draw on other leadership styles depending on the issue they are working through. These styles include instructional leader, servant leader, and adaptive leader. Effective leaders of teacher professional learning employ these three styles at different phases in their improvement work. Collectively, they have the power to define, implement, respond to, and maintain changes that bring about improved teaching expertise and, in turn, sustainable school improvement. Each has a distinct purpose, but when used together, they complement each other to support the development and implementation of effective pedagogical practices. In Table 2.1, we briefly define each of the leadership styles before offering key characteristics associated with each for you to consider within your own leadership practice.

Leading With an Adaptive Stance

Adaptive leaders actively look to empower their colleagues – not as a form of distributed managerialism in which teachers

TABLE 2.1 Leadership Styles

LEADERSHIP STYLE	KEY PURPOSE FOR LEADING TEACHER LEARNING
Adaptive leadership	To empower teaching teams to respond to complexity through incremental, iterative improvement practices. An adaptive leader promotes responsive implementation and uses **formative evidence** to drive expertise development.
Servant leadership	To be responsive to contextual needs by removing impediments to teacher learning. A servant leader strives to build an enabling environment that allows teachers to focus on their professional learning needs.
Instructional leadership	To promote and participate in teacher learning and development. An instructional leader is curious about and deeply engaged in dialogue about effective teaching and learning practices.

are burdened with administrative tasks, but as a way to raise the level of autonomy and responsibility of those they work with. This is expressed through specific behaviors, such as encouraging teachers to express opinions and ideas, promoting collaborative decision-making, and supporting information sharing and teamwork (Chen et al., 2011).

Adaptive leaders seek to mobilize knowledge quickly, are responsive to contextual needs, and seek to empower their colleagues to act – even when the path is unclear and the journey might be messy. Due to this, an adaptive school is able to respond swiftly to rapidly changing opportunities and demands as they occur, making it more efficient and effective in addressing the learning needs of its students.

Leading adaptive processes is an alternative to more traditional top-down management styles. Adaptive leadership is an approach that helps teams respond to unpredictability through incremental, repeated learning practices. At its core, adaptive approaches use an iterative structure consisting of short, focused learning cycles. During an iterative learning cycle, teams define the work, ensure the planned work takes place through daily interactions and routines, reflect on what has been undertaken and the utility of the intervention, and ultimately measure the merit of the design before moving through another iteration. Adaptive teams have a relentless focus on improving teaching practice and the achievement of the students they teach. They are committed to working in collaborative improvement cycles using evidence-informed approaches that meet contextual needs. (For further details on specific improvement structures to support the implementation of adaptive practices, see Chapter 1.) While working closely with leaders who display adaptive leadership practices, we developed the following characteristics to describe the way they work. Consider these characteristics, and compare them to how you currently lead school-improvement work.

Key Characteristics of Adaptive Leaders

- Encourage teaching teams to be responsive to the specific needs of their students

- Display humility by seeking to learn from different viewpoints and opinions

- Willingly adjust plans and strategies in response to formative evidence, rather than sticking to what was predicted

- Create an environment to test school-improvement ideas though short action and learning cycles

- Emphasize the importance of focusing on the school's long-term vision by promoting action-oriented behavior (What are we doing now to work toward long-term goals?)

- Personally invest in school-improvement work

Utilizing Servant Leadership Principles

Servant leadership can be quite a polarizing term, as it certainly engenders a power shift in which it is a school leader's job to serve all within the community. However, this would be a simplistic interpretation of a servant leader, and one fraught with danger of burnout for school leaders pulled in many directions under the guise of serving their community.

A servant leader is more accurately depicted as a leader who is continually looking for impediments that may hinder the growth of his or her teaching teams and endeavoring to remove these obstacles. A servant leader understands that for teacher learning to occur, there is a need for processes and structures that allow teacher learning to flourish. This leadership style strives to build the "enabling conditions" by removing barriers to teacher collaboration and growth.

A servant leader exhibits practices such as deep listening, self-awareness, and commitment to others. He or she does not direct the team by telling team members what to do. Instead, he or she supports the team to make rapid progress by helping them self-organize and make decisions that are responsive to their context and based on evidence. The enabling conditions need to be in place for this to occur. Servant leaders do not shift all responsibility to teachers and will take part in decision-making processes, and they can still voice disagreements, but they view one of their primary roles as supporting teachers to be able to do the work they need to do. This is achieved by empowering teams of teachers to respond to their context and their students.

In taking a holistic approach, servant leaders understand that social and emotional factors are inherent among any teaching staff. The servant leader's objective is to increase teamwork and personal agency over the improvement initiatives. This type of leader endeavors to create a participative environment, empowering teachers by sharing decision-making and distributing leadership. A servant leader is not ruler of the team but someone who is adept at encouraging, enabling, and energizing people to jell as a team and realize their full potential (www.scrum.org). By focusing on the needs of team members and those they serve, servant leaders support their teaching workforce to achieve results in line with the school's strategic intent. A servant leader will influence behaviors by modeling collaboration, trust, empathy, and ethical use of power.

Servant leadership is integral to adaptability and continuous improvement. To consider your current capabilities in this area, examine your current practices against the following characteristics.

Key Characteristics of Servant Leaders

- Focus on building a foundation of trust and psychological safety
- Stimulate group and individual empowerment and transparency
- Encourage and resource collaborative structures
- Convey empathy and listen deeply
- Display humility and situational awareness

Applying Instructional Leadership Approaches

Instructional leaders are involved in classroom observations, review and interpret assessment information with staff, have a clear mission about learning gains, communicate high expectations about achievement, and attend to opportunities to learn and ensure that the school environment is conducive to learning. Because they have a more direct involvement in teacher professional learning, they can nurture and embed learning processes that develop teachers' capabilities focused on improvement in teaching practice. Instructional leaders are curious about and deeply engaged in dialogue about what effective teaching and learning practices look like in their schools.

Robinson (2010) argued that the highest impact of school leaders was related to their promoting and participating in teacher learning and development. High-impact behaviors include planning, coordinating, evaluating teaching and the curriculum, establishing goals and expectations, strategic resourcing, collective efficacy about impact, and ensuring an orderly and supportive environment.

An instructional leader has a relentless focus on teaching and learning. This type of leader works to establish a high degree of consistency by planning, implementing, and establishing clear descriptions of practice. The clear descriptions of practice are focused on high-probability strategies that have the potential to significantly influence student learning. Instructional leaders articulate these practices as an expertise pathway where teachers at varying levels of experience can establish what is an appropriate next level of work.

Let's take, for example, a teacher who works at a school with a focus on classroom discourse. According to research, classroom discourse has the potential to considerably accelerate student learning, with a reported effect size of 0.82 (Hattie, 2009). This is well above the average effect size of 0.4. In other words, classroom discourse is a high-probability strategy that is worth pursuing. However, a focus on promoting discussion and dialogue in the classroom is still too broad a definition for an improvement effort – for example, an appropriate next level of work for a teacher whose classroom is worksheet-driven with little dialogue will be completely different from an appropriate next level of work for a teacher who has embedded Socratic questioning techniques. This is not about judging a teacher's practice as effective or ineffective; it is about supporting teachers to conceptualize a pathway they can work through as they develop their expertise within an area. (For in-depth descriptions of how instructional leaders can co-construct expertise pathways, see Chapter 3.)

Hattie and Smith (2020) outlined the major ways instructional leaders think and act. They argued that the most effective instructional school leaders think in ways quite different from leaders who have the least impact and influence.

Key Characteristics of Instructional Leaders

- Understand the need to focus on learning and the impact of teaching

- Believe their fundamental task is to evaluate the effect of everyone in their school on student learning

- Interpret successes and failures in student learning as directly related to what teachers and leaders did or didn't do

- See themselves as change agents

- Approach assessment as feedback about their impact

- Understand the importance of dialogue and of listening to student and teacher voices

- Set challenging targets for themselves and for teachers, to maximize student outcomes

- Welcome errors and share learning from their own missteps

- Create safe and high-trust environments in which teachers and students can learn from errors without losing face

(Hattie, 2015)

DISCUSSION QUESTIONS

- How adaptive is your school context?

- How do you currently position your school-improvement work – is it more about implementation with fidelity or implementation as learning? Is the focus on technical problems or adaptive challenges?

- What do you believe it would take to lead sustained teacher learning in your unique context?

- What type of school leader do you feel you are most of the time: instructional, servant, or adaptive? Do you consciously move between leadership styles depending on what is required?

CHAPTER 3

Evaluative Thinking and Expertise Pathways

When we examine how complex problems are successfully solved in other industries, it is evident that an evaluative stance is essential. Take, for example, the work of engineers when problem-solving; they hypothesize about the problem, they seek and utilize evidence, and they pursue probable solutions, often through experiments and simulations. Engineers need to have confidence in the identified solution and rely on industry evidence to support solutions to an identified problem. The very notion of evidence-informed practice has at its core an evaluative stance. While evidence-informed practice is based on empirical evidence, it acknowledges there is a local contextual element to implementation of what works. What works in one classroom does not always work in another classroom; as educators, we need to continually review the efficacy of any instructional strategies that have been introduced.

In education, the process of mobilizing research knowledge into effective teaching practices is also a complex chain of activities, requiring critique, synthesis, contextual factors, and implementation all working together (Sharples, 2013). Due to the intricate nature of practice improvement, it is essential to have systems for continual formative evaluation to establish whether benefits are realized, and there must be mechanisms to respond and adapt to emerging evidence in a timely manner.

A key underpinning principle to be able to respond and adapt is not only for practices to be clearly defined, but also for practices to be articulated with increasing levels of sophistication. We refer to this as an *expertise pathway*. Articulating increasing levels of sophistication will better place teachers to develop their expertise as they become more adept at the practice, and it will give leaders the ability to respond based on where teachers are situated within an expertise pathway.

Consider an implementation strategy based on learning intentions and success criteria. An expertise pathway might begin with a teacher exploring ways of clearly articulating to students what they should be able to know, do, and understand. But as a teacher deepens his or her expertise in relation to learning intentions, he or she would also begin to explore practices about how it is essential to effectively connect learning intentions to students' prior knowledge, as well as consider opportunities for co-constructing learning intentions with students to increase their ownership and agency. A teacher may also recognize the importance of developing his or her practices that link the formative assessment and feedback cycle to learning intentions. It would then be natural to move into practices related to scaffolding peer feedback or student self-regulation. The point is that practices such as learning intentions may appear quite simple to implement; however, truly supporting expertise development requires a considerable level of sophistication.

RESEARCH EVIDENCE: EVALUATIVE THINKING

Illustrating that professional learning translates into gains in student achievement poses tremendous challenges, despite an intuitive and logical connection (Borko, 2004; Loucks-Horsley & Matsumoto, 1999; Supovitz, 2001). Yoon et al. (2007) noted that "even if professional development enhances teacher knowledge and skills and improves classroom instruction, a poorly designed evaluation or inadequate implementation would make it difficult to detect any effects from the professional development" (p. 4).

Evaluative thinking has recently gained an increased emphasis in education and is now discussed as one of the key competencies of school leaders (Centre for Educational Statistics and Evaluation, 2015; Rickards et al., 2021). Evaluative thinking is a systematic reflective process that manifests as regular questioning, evidence seeking, and learning and developing an informed position – a clear chain of reasoning that connects the grounds, reasons, or evidence to an evaluative conclusion (Schwandt, 2008). It is increasingly viewed as an integral part of any school-improvement strategy. In fact, if improvement is not viewed through an evaluative lens, it will become very difficult to respond and adapt throughout the improvement journey as evidence emerges.

Amabile and Kramer (2011) noted that "of all the things that can boost emotions, motivation, and perceptions during a workday, the single most important is making progress in meaningful work" (p. 22). A key notion of meaningful work for teachers is knowing they have a positive impact on student learning. Regularly collecting and reviewing evidence of student learning with teachers and making progress visible is vitally important for sustained motivation.

Effective school leaders support teachers in their "meaningful work," by cueing them into monitoring progress through positive feedback loops. Amabile and Kramer (2011) concluded that if leaders "facilitate their steady progress salient to them [teachers], and treat them well, they will experience the emotions, motivations, and perceptions necessary for great performance. Their superior work will contribute to organizational success. And here's the beauty of it: They will love their jobs" (p. 80). Fullan (2011) echoed this claim: "It is the actual experience of being more effective that spurs [people] to repeat and build on the behavior" (p. 52). Without an evaluative lens, none of this will come to fruition.

With this in mind, it is essential that school leaders have a clear sense of what would constitute evidence of impact. Unless there is clarity about what kind of data clearly demonstrates improvement, then it will be impossible to undertake rigorous improvement work underpinned by ongoing formative evaluation. By articulating the complex chain of improvement activities and identifying what would constitute evidence of impact, leaders can begin to identify critical levels they are striving to achieve.

School leaders need to also consider that the linear nature of traditional evaluation approaches does not necessarily fit well with the complexity of school-improvement work. Rapidly changing contexts require evaluation approaches that are fluid and responsive, in order to address issues of complexity, connectivity, and change as innovation unfolds (Gopalakrishnan et al., 2013). Educational evaluation, in simplistic terms, involves the systematic collection, analysis, and interpretation of evidence to inform decisions and identify the effects of an educational initiative (Earl & Timperley, 2015). School-improvement work should have a dual focus that seeks to generate new practices to explore while carefully considering what evidence of impact would look like. Evaluative thinking involves a continuous cycle of generating hypotheses, taking action, collecting formative evidence, and continually reflecting on progress. It encourages those involved to experiment, make mistakes, and consider where they are, using a fresh and independent review of the course and the effects of the innovation (Earl & Timperley, 2015).

Earl and Timperley (2015) defined evaluative thinking as an *iterative and dynamic process* in which evaluators support innovators to:

- define and describe the innovation and its evolution,
- identify the purpose(s) of the innovation and the expected outcomes,
- frame evaluation questions,
- collect and analyze evidence,
- interpret evidence gathered from multiple stakeholder groups across different contexts, and
- share insights and findings.

PRINCIPLES AND PRACTICES

It is the intention of "leaders as evaluators" (Hattie & Clinton, 2011) to understand the influence that everyone in their school has on the progress of students. Focus questions that dominate their leadership include the following:

- How do we know this is working?
- How can we compare this practice with that one?
- What is the merit and worth of this as it relates to various learning processes and outcomes?
- What is the magnitude of this improvement work?
- Where is the evidence that shows that this is superior to other options?
- Where have we seen this practice implemented so that it produces effective results?

In essence, an evaluative leader is working in the same way as a classroom teacher when that teacher is examining his or her impact on students. The expert teacher sets out to develop a common understanding and shared language around what success looks like in the classroom, as a way to determine whether students are learning and what the next steps should be. Essentially, the mantra of "knowing thy impact" entails connecting what teachers do with what learners learn. To lead with an evaluative mindset means to ensure improvement practices are fine-grained enough for teachers to implement and practise before moving on to new levels of expertise. It also means finding ways to conduct real-time checks for understanding, just as a classroom teacher would, so that appropriate support and challenge is available for all teachers.

By working through evaluative processes as a group, teachers and leaders will have time and space to consider how they are thinking. This is particularly important for identifying and unlearning ineffective habits. For example, the simple question "What makes you think that?" prompts us to explain how we formed our judgments, including the evidence that helped us arrive at our conclusions. Drawing conclusions based on intuition or instinct is not evaluative thinking and will ultimately lead to consistently poorer decisions. It is essential that we develop our ability to make informed decisions based on the evidence of practice improvement and implementation. As such, evaluative thinking becomes an essential element to reframe teaching and learning from an evidence-informed perspective.

> It is essential that we develop our ability to make informed decisions based on the evidence of practice improvement and implementation.

To support teachers to deepen their expertise, school leaders must nurture them to continually deepen their knowledge of teaching and learning by engaging with research evidence and honing their evaluative thinking skills. To achieve this, school leaders should strive to create an environment where this is possible by modeling the evaluative thinking they wish to develop in their teachers.

Evaluative school leaders are able to identify key areas of focus for improvement, be deliberate and intentional with implementation, be problem-solvers and hypothesis-testers, be cognizant of their impact on teachers, and be active in seeking second opinions.

Defining Practices to Support Improvement

Effective school-program evaluation does more than collect, analyze, and present data. It makes it possible for school leaders to gather useful information, to appropriately translate these data into action, and to continually learn about the improvement strategies in place. To formatively evaluate practice improvement, it is essential that you establish a clear picture of how your school or team will undertake its improvement work. In other words, you must determine the key resources, activities, outcomes, and connections that will underpin the implementation strategy – that is, you must design an expertise pathway.

The purpose of an expertise pathway is to provide a road map describing a plausible sequence of related activities, artifacts, and processes that would lead to the improvement strategy's desired results. Mapping a proposed expertise pathway helps you visualize and understand how specific actions taken in the classroom could lead to specific outcomes and evidence of impact. Teams can co-construct an expertise pathway where they begin to map out what teaching practices might look like as they become increasingly adept at the practice. This exercise will ensure team discussions are focused on the specific practices that could lead to improved outcomes.

Developing an expertise pathway is about articulating the causal chain of events you would expect to see. You might view it as a set of cause-and-effect relationships that connect the parts within the pathway to each other: "If we do *this*, then we should expect to see *that*." This critical stage in school-improvement work is about designing a clear picture of how an improvement strategy is connected to and relies on many other smaller actions, resources, and processes of a given expertise pathway.

Articulating Expertise Pathways

Creating an expertise pathway requires systematic thinking and planning to be able to construct an implementation strategy. In addition, while the expertise pathway is an implementation blueprint, it should be flexible in allowing school teams to be responsive to different context-specific scenarios. With a well-designed expertise pathway, you can adjust approaches and alter courses of action as plans emerge and formative evidence is collected and analyzed. Formative evidence includes teacher observations, listening to students' feedback about their learning, and artifacts of student work (assignments, assessments) collected and importantly evaluatively interpreted during the course of the lesson or series of lessons (summative evidence is similar information that is collected at the end, but could well be used formatively to inform the next series of lessons; a key point here is that "formative" or "summative" is a quality not of the evidence itself but of when it is collected and interpreted).

The expertise pathway is about establishing clarity about a hypothesized implementation journey, ongoing formative assessment, critical review, and thoughtful adjustments that will lead to the most optimal results.

Utilizing evaluative-thinking techniques and developing a logical expertise pathway will lead to greater learning opportunities, improved documentation of and success in achieving outcomes that matter, and a shared knowledge about *what* works best in your context and *why*. Collaboratively conceptualizing an expertise pathway that underpins an improvement strategy is a beneficial evaluation technique that will enable and simplify effective program planning, implementation, and formative and summative evidence. When these different groups contribute to the evaluative-thinking processes, their combined perspectives create the space for new insights and breakthroughs in learning (Earl & Timperley, 2015).

In essence, an expertise pathway is a systematic and visual way to represent a group understanding of the relationships among the many and varied teaching practices involved in the improvement work. Once a clear picture of the practices that should lead to improvement has been established, you can carefully consider the types of evidence you would expect to see as a result of implementing the practices. Key points to consider are that articulating an expertise pathway is meant to be feasible within your context, to be practical so that you can begin implementing with specificity, and to contain levels of sophistication that cater for a range of expertise levels within your school.

The purpose of an expertise pathway is to shift improvement thinking from the implicit to the explicit, thus giving voice to the often-unrecognized assumptions that guide our improvement work. This will help detect any lack of consensus among team members and reveal any weakness or incoherence in the proposed improvement logic (Davidoff et al., 2015).

> The purpose of an expertise pathway is to shift improvement thinking from the implicit to the explicit.

An expertise pathway is a critical technique for school leaders, for three strategic reasons:

- *Developing a moral imperative* underpins the improvement work.

    Any improvement initiative should be underpinned by an improvement story. The moral imperative is essential, because it drives *why* you are doing the work, not just *what* you seek to do and *how* you intend to do it. The underlying *why* is essential to motivate and sustain improvement efforts, particularly when you are working in a complex environment bound to present challenges. A moral imperative gives people a bigger reason to continue to push forward when things get tough. Firmly grounding the moral imperative in the needs of students, so that you clearly state *why* there is a driving need to focus on specific practices, becomes a key driver for improvement.

- *Describing the improvement journey as an expertise pathway* supports the development of shared agency within the groups involved in its creation.

    The language used to chronicle the journey should be clear and specific enough to be widely understood by those involved in implementation. By collectively focusing attention and resources, the school will also be better able to formatively monitor improvement (or lack thereof).

- *Adapting over time as you learn more* is a core idea when developing an expertise pathway.

    Although an expertise pathway may begin as a snapshot in time – how you hypothesize the journey will unfold – it should always be viewed as a work in progress, and teams should intend to refine and update it as they learn more through the improvement journey. The expertise pathway will drive what formative evidence is collected and how you to intend to analyze it.

An effective school leader exhibits evaluative thinking and is prepared to publicize the successes (or setbacks) the school is having with regard to student learning. Specifying key milestones as an expertise pathway will position the school to design an improvement strategy that allows the team to collect and analyze evidence periodically throughout the journey. As you move into implementation and exhibit an evaluative mindset through formative evidence collection and analysis, it will become possible to recognize problems early and respond to them in a timely manner. Your expertise pathway is a hypothesized path, and it should be viewed as adaptive. Be prepared to make course corrections and adjustments as you collaboratively collect, interpret, and consider emerging evidence.

STORY FROM THE FIELD

To provide a clear sense of what an expertise pathway looks like in practice, we thought it would be beneficial to explore an illustrative example of how one elementary school approached this when seeking to develop mathematics teaching expertise. When considering this example, keep in mind the many ways other schools and districts could have approached this area of focus. Current teaching practices, school context, curriculum, professional learning structures, and so on will all play a part in what the most appropriate expertise pathway might be for your school. There is not necessarily one pathway that will lead to success; what is important is that the pathway be evidence-informed, that the sequence be logical for your context, and that the connections between each step be understood by those expected to implement it.

This particular expertise pathway focuses on a strategy for improving students' ability to reason mathematically by focusing on classroom discourse. Classroom discourse is an instructional strategy shown to help students learn and understand content (Fisher et al., 2016). Globally, mathematics curricula now require teachers to explicitly teach and assess key proficiencies and mathematical practices such as problem-solving, reasoning, and critical thinking (Australian Curriculum, Assessment and Reporting Authority, 2018; Common Core State Standards Initiative, 2011). Added to this, mathematics educators are hearing recommendations that it is no longer enough to require students to "do mathematics." Rather, there is an increasing demand that students be able to demonstrate an ability to think, behave, and communicate mathematically (Boaler, 2008a, b). As a result, classroom discussion has been viewed as an appropriate instructional strategy to support the cultivation of mathematical practices in which students are able to "justify their answers and critique the reasoning of others" (Common Core State Standards Initiative, 2011). These practices are based on what are considered essential "processes and proficiencies" with long-standing importance in mathematics education (Symons & Dunn, 2019). Yet knowing the research basis supporting classroom discourse and establishing its grounding in mathematics curriculum does not necessarily give teachers implementable steps to develop their expertise in this area. That's why we suggest building expertise pathways: to articulate implementable steps that should lead to a deepening of sophistication and expertise over time.

The following Story From the Field is from Amelia Eldridge, a deputy principal at Cowra Public School, describing the journey her school undertook when implementing an expertise pathway in mathematics.

Cowra Public School

By Amelia Eldridge, instructional leader

▶ In 2020, Cowra Public School, a rural primary school in New South Wales, Australia, implemented dedicated teacher professional learning time into the teaching timetable. Each Thursday, stage groups (fortnightly rotation) were released from face-to-face teaching to meet together for two hours to engage in targeted professional learning. This professional learning was flexible and aligned with whole-school, cohort, and individual teacher needs. Building professional learning into the timetable showed that teachers' own learning was highly valued and prioritized. Time was given to allow teachers to engage in professional discourse and collaboration around learning, to analyze student data, and to program and reflect on their teaching practices.

A specific example of how Cowra Public School has used this professional learning model to drive improvement is in the area of mathematics. It was noted through both internal and external data sources that students were struggling to efficiently and effectively work mathematically, communicate, reason, and problem-solve.

In 2019, an instructional routine, Number Talks, was introduced into classrooms to encourage students to articulate and explain their reasoning around the use of strategies when solving mathematical problems. Teachers used specific instructional techniques (talk moves) to encourage students to engage in structured conversation on mathematics concepts and to gain insights into how students solved problems. The implementation of this framework gave teachers practical techniques to develop whole-class discussion and to begin to elicit the way the students were reasoning mathematically. However, teachers also felt that they needed to deepen the sophistication of the work as they became comfortable with the practices associated with "talk

(Continued)

(Continued)

moves." The teachers were looking for a pathway they could follow as their expertise developed.

The following year, Cowra Public School was given the opportunity to participate in an online professional learning initiative with the purpose of improving language and literacy outcomes in mathematics. A key aspect of this program was to articulate an expertise pathway that was appropriate for the context you were working in. This program built on the work we commenced in 2019 and discussed that if students are to acquire mathematical language, they must be explicitly taught how to talk in a productive and meaningful way. So, the expertise pathway was not just about "talk"; it also needed to include a specific focus on the type of language that was to be used (the key mathematical terms we wanted students to use); valuing talk by developing success criteria related to talk; developing a knowledge of mathematical reasoning and the types of questions teachers could ask to elicit different forms of reasoning; and, finally, exploring instructional routines such as number strings that enable meaningful discussion to take place.

The hypothesized pathway we followed is shown in Figure 3.1.

FIGURE 3.1

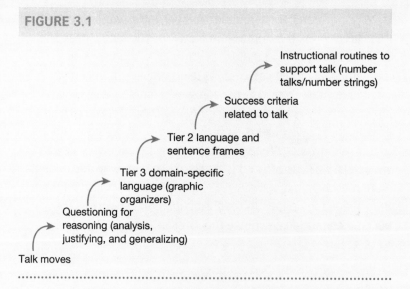

DEVELOPING TEACHING EXPERTISE

The implementation of this pathway across the whole school ensured common language and practices in all classrooms. The professional development was delivered in incremental steps across the academic year, to ensure that levels on the expertise pathway were explored in depth, with the school's instructional leader supporting the development of key actions individual teachers would take. For each step in the pathway, we would undertake a key reading based on the practice about to be explored, meet for periodic review throughout the incremental step, and then reconvene for a review of the learning we undertook. Each step in the pathway highlighted key instructional practices teachers could undertake; clear ideas about artifacts to collect, to determine the impact of the practice; and a reflective piece, to ensure teachers considered their personal learning journey.

As instructional leader, I found that the delivery of this particular professional development not only supported teachers to introduce a new strategy to increase student talk, but also inspired and supported teachers to develop an authentic reflective framework in which to consider their own practice and share insights with their cohort. A key idea for the expertise pathway was to "learn a little, try a little," and teachers embraced this mantra, as it afforded them the opportunity to experiment, adjust, modify, and take risks.

Prior to the delivery of the theory and evidence-based practice for each step of the professional learning journey, teachers were required to video themselves during a particular explicit teaching session. Some teachers were very comfortable with watching and reflecting on their practice in this way; others were challenged, but all could see the value and authenticity in the process. Teachers' comments as they watched their own videos included "I thought I was asking open questions, but I tend to revert to closed very quickly" and "Students are beginning to use the vocabulary in their conversations."

(Continued)

(Continued)

The gradual delivery of instructional routines during the four modules gave teachers the necessary understanding of how and why the routine developed mathematical language and discourse but also the time to practise, refine, and reflect on each routine.

As instructional leader, I was able to co-plan, co-teach, and co-reflect with individual teachers as they implemented the practices. Through providing explicit feedback, I was able to help teachers consolidate their understandings and embed routine into their teaching of mathematics in order to ultimately improve students' use of mathematical language. It became clear that breaking an improvement initiative down into manageable steps was an effective way to support classroom-level implementation and understanding.

ACTION ITEM: DESIGN AN EXPERTISE PATHWAY

The purpose of an expertise pathway is to provide those embarking on school-improvement work with a road map of related activities, artifacts, and processes that will lead to the desired results. Mapping a proposed pathway will not only enable the team to visualize and understand the specific areas of expertise development, but also highlight the evidence needed to gather insight about the improvement initiative.

The first step in this process is to acknowledge the fact that, as a team, you are committing to articulating your improvement work and the fact that, by doing this, you will end up with a more refined version of your improvement plan. An expertise pathway helps identify the factors that will affect your implementation plan and enable you to anticipate what evidence of impact will look like. As you collaboratively create your expertise pathway, your school will be required to systematically explore important planning, implementation, and formative-evaluation issues, such as the following.

Define the Practice

There is no doubt that improvement work can stumble and sometimes fail due to a lack of clarity about what we need to do. As such, school-improvement processes need to move beyond broad definitions. David Hopkins highlighted the idea that "unless you define practice and make it common you can't improve the quality of teaching." While it may seem like common sense, this part of the process is vitally important. Developing and capturing a shared understanding is a priority for successful implementation and improvement. Teachers, school leaders, and other key stakeholders should collaboratively generate an agreed understanding of what the practice could look like in their context at this point in time.

Take formative assessment, for example. Many different practices fit within this broad term. However, if we begin to define an implementation strategy that refines "formative assessment" further to Dylan Williams's notion of "responsive teaching," we can begin to think more clearly about specific techniques that would support teachers to respond to students' understanding. Clearly defining the practice up front allows us to consider specific techniques that would align with the definition. For the example of responsive teaching, a school might explore techniques such as turn and talk, cold calling, "show me" boards, hinge questions, and exit slips, to name a few.

Collaboratively Construct an Expertise Pathway

When focusing on student learning, Rosenshine (2010) highlighted that if students are presented with too much information at one time, they become confused, as they are unable to process it all. Adult learners, including teachers, are just as likely as young students to experience working-memory overload if they are confronted with too much information at once. So, it is logical to break complex teaching practices and improvement strategies into manageable steps.

The added benefit of breaking instructional practice down into manageable steps is that we are creating precise specifications of the practices we seek to improve. For classroom observation to be effective, teams of teachers need to have a shared understanding of what high-quality instruction looks like. Co-constructing precise specifications of practice that outline examples of practice will allow teachers to explore instruction with precision. Precise specifications of practice in an expertise pathway serve three purposes:

1. The co-construction phase enables a shared understanding to be defined and articulated.

2. Specifications of practice support classroom implementation by making practice examples clear and transparent.

3. The specificity allows for focused observation to take place linked to instructional goals.

Unless you specify how these practices can be incrementally established in an expertise pathway over time, the improvement journey can quickly become susceptible to sweeping statements (about improving feedback, differentiation, engagement, etc.) that leave everyone confused about what the practices actually look like in the classroom and how the team could deepen their expertise over time.

Expertise pathways should be co-designed by groups of teachers and take into account educational research, teachers' professional knowledge, and school context. When different groups contribute to the evaluative-thinking processes, their combined perspectives create the space for new insights and breakthroughs in learning (Earl & Timperley, 2015). The involvement of different people within the school community will lead to not only a deeper shared understanding of the work, but also a deeper commitment to it.

Teaching is complex, and there is a range of ways we can approach improvement in teaching practices. Indeed, it is worthwhile to think about "differentiated" teaching, as no one method may work for all students, and certainly when re-teaching an idea it may be critical to use a different method – if it did not work the first time, why would you expect it to work if repeated? What's important is that you create a specific description about the practices you are seeking to improve and establish clarity around how teachers can become increasingly sophisticated at implementing them in the classroom. By doing this, you will be in a position to deliberately and intentionally build teaching expertise over time.

Formative Evaluation That Enables Real-Time Monitoring and Adjustment

There are two major types of evaluation questions: (1) formative questions that help improve the implementation of your improvement strategy and (2) summative questions that establish whether your improvement strategy worked the way you planned. Both are important, but we often minimize formative questions, which are essential to refine improvement work while we are deep in it and there is still time to make the necessary adjustments for success. Lessons learned from early implementation are critical for broader implementation success. Formative evidence becomes essential to support decision making on key aspects such as scaling improvement work within your school.

To illustrate what this might look like in practice, carefully consider formative evaluation and evidence collection. This begs the question: What key evidence checkpoints could provide insights into the level of expertise development that is occurring? Your first instinct might be to capture specific classroom practices as they take place, which is definitely a useful form of evidence, but this may also be difficult to schedule and result in practices that are not truly reflective of what normally happens in the classroom. So, while capturing classroom practice is definitely a worthwhile pursuit, there are also many other insights to be gained from broadening the type of evidence you collect in an effort to continually learn about and refine the improvement strategy while it is being implemented.

For example, while learning walks (explored in Chapter 1) are a useful mechanism for sharing exemplary practice, they can also be a useful way to collect evidence on any school-improvement strategy. The first thing to note with a learning walk is that it differs from instructional rounds (also explored in Chapter 1) in scope and formality. Unlike instructional rounds – which use protocols for establishing long-term networks, defining problems of practice, and formally analyzing patterns – learning walks are more loosely structured (Fisher & Frey, 2014). The other important aspect is that a learning walk should involve teachers, so that as you work toward school-wide adoption of practices, teachers have the opportunity to observe what is taking place in a range of classrooms.

One way of introducing learning walks can be to undertake what Fisher and Frey (2014) described as a *ghost walk*. In a ghost walk, teachers walk through classrooms with no students present, so the discussion is confined to the physical environment. The scope of the walk should be clearly defined, so that teachers are aware of what the visitors will be looking for: a specific part of the expertise pathway. Observable artifacts of learning could be the way the classroom is set out, the anchor charts and co-constructed worked examples that are used to scaffold student understanding, and so forth.

As trust is built through the use of ghost walks, learning walks can evolve into capacity-building walks (Fisher & Frey, 2014) in which teachers are involved in the observation and collection of evidence of impact. As with the ghost walk, you should define clear boundaries about the specific practices for which you are intending to collect evidence. The intention of a capacity-building learning walk is to gather formative evidence of teaching practices that can inform future implementation decisions. For mathematics classroom discourse, these might include auditing the range of talk moves teachers use, exploring whether students invite comments from their classmates and build on each other's ideas, analyzing whether teacher questions elicit different forms of reasoning, or capturing whether students use tier 3 language when communicating mathematically.

Whether doing a ghost walk or capacity-building walk, the key is to ensure they are performed consistently so that formative evidence can be gathered, interpreted, and used to inform future action.

DISCUSSION QUESTIONS

- How well do you currently define the key practices you are seeking to improve?

- What would need to be in place to develop precise specifications of practice articulated as an expertise pathway? How could these be collaboratively developed?

- Does evaluative thinking underpin your improvement work?

- What mechanisms do you currently have in place to collect formative impact evidence, and how do you use it to drive next steps in your implementation journey?

CHAPTER 4

Adaptive Teaching Teams and Collaborative Expertise

In schools, the majority of professional learning structures suggest teachers work on focus areas in collaboration with colleagues. This is due to a large body of research that argues professional learning and expertise development can be more effective if teachers work as a group (Cordingley, 2015; Desimone, 2009; Dunst & Hamby, 2015; Timperley et al., 2007; Walter & Briggs, 2012; Wei et al., 2009). Collaborative processes enable exploratory conversations in which teachers challenge each other and have an opportunity to clarify misunderstandings to arrive at workable solutions for their classroom.

However, Sims and Fletcher-Wood (2020) recently challenged the notion that collaboration is the key factor. They highlighted that collaboration does not guarantee group professional learning interventions will lead to improved pupil achievement. We agree with this sentiment, as simply putting teachers together does not ensure improvement will occur. Hargreaves (1994) has long warned against contrived collegiality. School leaders need to also be clear about *how* and *why* collaboration is useful if it is to lead to meaningful impact on teaching and learning. Collaboration needs to be linked to what we know from the behavioral sciences about how learning occurs. Collaboration linked with cycles of action and review, in which teachers have opportunities to practise explicit aspects of their practice that have been defined clearly and modeled for them, are also important for expertise to not only develop, but also be sustained.

> School leaders need to also be clear about *how* and *why* collaboration is useful if it is to lead to meaningful impact on teaching and learning.

RESEARCH EVIDENCE

Creating a School Culture to Respond to Complexity

The very idea of effectively developing teaching expertise can be elusive, even within an industry such as education that has learning at its core. To complicate matters further, this all takes place against a backdrop of increasing diversity and complexity that school leadership teams must face. Catering to individual teachers' needs while balancing the needs of the collective group of teachers is a challenge that needs careful consideration when you are designing a professional learning framework for teachers in your school.

When designing collaborative teacher professional learning, leaders should understand that they can create shared mental models among team members, and that these team mental models are an essential underlying mechanism of effective team processes and performance (Marks et al., 2000). Team mental models are established by taking the time to build the way the team works to a point where team members begin to organize and interpret information in a similar manner – they have an established way of working and thinking.

Research on individual decision-making processes and the difference between experts and novices has long recognized the critical role that individual mental models play in the interpretation of new information. This is also the case when we consider collaborative expertise and team mental models. Deliberately and intentionally cultivating teams that have a shared understanding of how to communicate, process information, and make informed decisions is critical when undertaking teacher professional learning in schools.

As teams develop shared mental models, they will begin to become more adept at processes such as communication, decision-making, and contextual awareness. Marks et al. (2000) found that leaders who spent time establishing group norms around interaction and routine ways of working can develop teams that have a sustained impact. Establishing these norms affected the development of mental models, which in turn positively influenced team communication processes and performance.

In fact, team mental models built around communication processes and decision-making strongly predicted performance when the teams encountered novel problems. In the context of this study, novel problems were defined as unfamiliar or unique situations that, although they may have the same core objectives as more familiar environments do, differ in terms of the specific practice required to lead to a workable solution. They were novel because there was some inherent ambiguity or unpredictability – the very essence of what Heifetz and Laurie (1997) described as adaptive challenges.

Due to the unpredictable nature and contextual factors inherent in teaching and schools, it is often impossible to prepare teams for every situation they will encounter in a classroom. Therefore, it is important that teams be responsive and adaptive to their unique context if they are to successfully impact teaching and learning. For this to happen, we need to consider how leaders can deliberately and intentionally develop team mental models.

During the role-establishment phase of team building, members who feel they have genuine agency over the work tend to interact productively with their colleagues to establish the nature and scope of each member's roles and expectations. Crucially, as roles and expectations are defined, they begin to develop a clear picture of how their unique knowledge, skills, and capabilities fit together, and how they can best utilize them to address problems (Katz & Kahn, 1978; Kozlowski et al., 1999). Once the team begins to shift its focus toward task execution, its mental models allow members to revise and refine the scope of work and to continuously improve performance (Pearsall et al., 2010). Continuous improvement is achieved by seeking formative impact evidence and reviewing this in teams, before responding with actionable next steps.

Coovert et al. (1996) argued that effective teams should be both adaptive and dynamic, meaning their behavior should be determined by team goals and the need to adapt to environmental conditions. Adaptive teaching teams with well-developed mental models are well-positioned to perform in environments that present problems different from previous experience or that require technical solutions other than what they may have applied in the past.

The Military, Complexity, and Adaptive Teams

Theory on how complex systems function can provide insights into the nature of adaptation and how it might operate at a

DEVELOPING TEACHING EXPERTISE

team level. The U.S. and Australian militaries, for example, have systematically developed more adaptive ways of working. While the strict, rigid nature we sometimes associate with the military might be true to a certain extent, it is also true the military realizes that inflexible adherence to rules and procedures can have catastrophic consequences on the battlefield (Menaker et al., 2006). Because the frontline environment is complex, military leaders understand that key contextual factors from the field should shape decision-making. Soldiers need to know the rules and procedure well enough to recognize when they may need to move outside of these and adapt to the context-specific situation. So, while the armed forces may not first appear to be a place from which educational leaders could learn and develop parallel practices, it may actually be fertile ground for the complexity we are experiencing in schools.

The Australian military considered adaptation in natural systems in an attempt to develop general principles of adaptation. The idea was to look to nature for inspiration, because nature has solved countless complex problems through adaptation. Grisogono and Radenovic (2007) suggested replacing the commonly used plan for military action – Observe, Orient, Decide, Act (OODA), developed by American military strategist Colonel John Boyd – with the Act, Sense, Decide, Adapt (ASDA) model. Grisogono and Radenovic (2011) were attempting to ensure the language of the model was accessible and recognizable to soldier-implementers. The shift from "act" to "adapt," while subtle, is important. "Act" can be viewed as a repetitive activity, whereas "adapt" explicitly recognizes the need to change. This approach assumes that the leader may not know what the perfect course of action is and must acquire information so the team can adapt their actions to correspond more directly with the context. This model has many connections to how educators can conceptualize implementing evidence-informed approaches in complex environments.

It should be noted that adaptation may not be as intuitive as we might like to think it is. Often the natural desire is to "set and forget" (Green, 2011). Humans tend to want to make decisions and then move on to the next problem. This may work well in a complicated environment, where cause and effect can be well defined, but not so well in a complex one, where exact predictions cannot be made. Complexity requires you to continually monitor how improvement is tracking.

Furthermore, by developing a framework with adaptation at the center, we are intentionally attempting to circumvent or counteract cognitive biases that invariably sneak into decision-making processes (Green, 2011). This is achieved by compelling leaders and team members to continually test their assumptions and knowledge in context-specific environments. Brookfield (2003) discussed how transformative experiences force us to confront the possibility that our beliefs may not actually fit. In this way, teachers and leaders will voluntarily, albeit sometimes reluctantly, critically evaluate their preconceived notions and practices.

PRINCIPLES AND PRACTICES
Cultivating Adaptive Ways of Working and Thinking

Adaptive teams are empowered to focus on the work they perceive as most important, providing them a higher level of agency and autonomy. The underlying premise is that being adaptive enables teams to focus on the key challenges they have identified, with an aim to build effective solutions through iterative testing and learning cycles. Teachers working in a supportive way to help each other improve, analyze student learning, plan, and problem-solve is a worthwhile goal to pursue. The underpinning idea is that the collaborative teacher team should be where evidence-informed teaching ideas are conceived and tested.

However, the team is also where interpersonal issues may arise and where group dynamics can hinder improvement rather than cultivate it. This social complexity of collaborative work means that cultivating effective teams is more complicated than simply scheduling groups of teachers to be together at a certain time. Educational leaders need to deliberately and intentionally support teachers to develop ways of working as an effective team, aiming their efforts toward a shared goal, task, or outcome. A common reflection we hear from leaders is that their teacher teams seem to be working *in* a group rather than working *as* a group. They have geographic proximity to each other, but this does necessarily ensure they work as a cohesive team in which there is positive inter-dependence and colleagues seek out and support each other to improve practices. Working *in* a group is what Hargreaves (1994) referred to as contrived collegiality – a situation where teachers in the same room may very well be positive and friendly, but they are not necessarily critically engaging with the work to achieve their goal collectively.

There are many reasons teams may not achieve a deep level of collegiality and collaboration. In our observation, some common reasons for this include the absence of trust, fear of conflict, lack of collective agency, or inattention to results, to name a few. In fact, for many people, working in a team can be a cause of stress rather than fulfillment. Consider a team in which the dynamic of the group is competitive. Rarely would this lead to improved knowledge or performance by the group members. So, while it is usually relatively easy to observe when a team is not functioning effectively, the more complex issue to tackle is how to support teacher teams to become effective working groups that lead to enhanced teaching expertise and, in turn, improved student outcomes.

WHAT DO WE KNOW ABOUT EFFECTIVE WORKING TEAMS?

► This is an area that Google researchers wanted to better understand when they embarked on Project Aristotle. Using input from executives across the globe, the research team identified 180 teams to study that included a mix of high- and low-performing teams. The study tested how both team composition (e.g., personality traits, demographics) and team dynamics (e.g., what it was like to work with teammates) impacted team effectiveness. The project pulled ideas from existing research as well as Google's own experience with what makes an effective team. The researchers found that what really mattered was less about who is on the team and more about how the team worked together. In order of importance, here are the traits that most influenced the effectiveness of a team:

- *Psychological safety*: Psychological safety refers to an individual's perception of the consequences of taking an interpersonal risk, or his or her belief that a team is safe for risk-taking (he or she will not be seen as ignorant, incompetent, negative, or disruptive). In a team with high psychological safety, teammates feel safe to take risks around their team members. They feel confident that no one on the team will embarrass or punish anyone else for admitting a mistake, asking a question, or offering a new idea.

- *Dependability*: On dependable teams, members reliably complete quality work on time and are not likely to shirk their responsibilities.

- *Structure and clarity*: It is important that each individual understand his or her job expectations, the process for fulfilling these expectations, and the consequences of his or her performance. Goals can be set at the individual and/or group level, but they must be specific, challenging, and attainable.

- *Meaning*: This relates to finding a sense of purpose in either the work itself or the output. The meaning of work is personal and can vary (e.g., financial security, supporting family, helping the team succeed, or self-expression) for each individual.

- *Impact*: Impact refers to the results of one's work; it is the subjective judgment that one's work is making a difference. Teams are more effective when each member can see that his or her work is contributing to the organization's goals.

(Re: Work with Google, n.d.)

Developing Collaborative Decision-Making and Collective Expertise

To support growth in individual practice and thereby better enable school improvement, leaders must also focus on the sophistication of the collaborative expertise of their teaching teams. For individuals, we know that "practice with purpose" (Deans for Impact, 2016) is an essential element for an individual to be able to develop mental model representations that guide decision-making. Through deliberate practice, expert teachers learn to make the right decision at the right time. Individual mental models allow teachers to self-monitor performance as a way to constantly improve their practice. School leaders should aspire for their teaching teams to also develop ways to self-monitor performance. This can be achieved through the development of team norms and ways of working – such as group communication, self-monitoring by collecting and analyzing impact evidence, decision-making processes, and moving the situation through action.

Many forms of teacher professional learning work within a collaborative framework (see Chapter 1 for specific structures). This allows for the de-privatization of teaching practice, encourages shared problem-solving, and enables discussion around student learning progress. The underlying principle is we can learn more together than we can working in isolation. In many ways, the concept of collaborative expertise has emerged from the research on individual expertise development and what we know about individual mental models. With this in mind, it becomes paramount that school leaders consider how to deliberately and intentionally develop the collaborative expertise of the teachers within their schools.

As such, we can begin to map out some key principles that underpin collaborative decision-making and collective expertise:

- *Empower teaching teams to focus on student learning.* Adaptive teams deliver high-quality, context-specific teaching and learning, with student needs driving the learning process. Teams should have time to understand the students and their needs. School leaders trust teaching teams to make informed decisions about the way they work and what they work on. The emphasis here is on implementing local, evidence-informed teaching and learning solutions that will promote student achievement.

- *Promote reflective dialogue and productive interactions.* Teachers can articulate why and how working in a team helps them develop more sophisticated responses to improvement work. For teams to succeed, teachers will need to exhibit skills such as encouraging colleagues to stretch their practice or share creative ideas, listening, clarifying, checking for understanding, and questioning. These interactive skills enhance communication, trust, leadership, decision-making, and conflict resolution.

- *Cultivate positive interdependence.* Teams should be built on the premise of collaboratively problem-solving instructional areas the team is grappling with. This is achieved by defining instructional practices clearly and designing an expertise pathway that would lead to improvement (see Chapter 3 for details on expertise pathways). An expertise pathway enables teachers to be connected to each other in accomplishing a common goal. Teams that apply iterative testing and learning strategies will use action to get unstuck, inspire thinking, and move toward group consensus.

- *Retain individual accountability.* Individual accountability means that as well as contributing to the group, each team member is responsible for demonstrating his or her own learning. Teachers who actively engage in collaborative work use it to process, extend, or apply learning for their individual needs. They value others' contributions but also take individual responsibility for actions taken in their classroom.

- *Monitor implementation and be responsive to emerging evidence.* Adaptive teaching teams should be responsive to what's actually best for students rather than what was predicted to be effective. As they develop understanding through testing and learning cycles, these teams will embrace new learning. Adaptive teams are curious about emerging evidence and seek to simplify practices as they deepen their understanding.

Although it is impossible to anticipate the precise dynamics of the future, cultivating adaptive teams should enable schools to adjust quickly to rapidly changing conditions and seize upon previously unforeseen opportunities. These attributes will be critical for every school and district to consider as we continue down this road of increased uncertainty.

STORY FROM THE FIELD

Dandenong High School, located in the southeast of Melbourne, is a co-educational setting from Years 7 to 12 with an enrollment of approximately 1,700 students. The school is highly multicultural, with sixty-two nationalities and eighty different language groups represented, and 89 percent of students speak a language other than English at home. The school's vision is to create an environment where every student can achieve success, and it does this by focusing on excellence and equity for all.

The following story explores the school's journey to develop a collaborative learning environment to support teacher professional learning. As you will see, it is an evolution that has taken place over five years and highlights the importance of building a culture in which teachers, leaders, and students are recognized as valued learners.

Building Collaborative Teaching Teams and Ensuring Practice Excellence at Dandenong High School
By Susan Ogden, principal

IDENTIFYING THE "PROBLEM OF PRACTICE"

In April 2015, I was sitting in a presentation by literacy specialist, grappling with how we were going to improve reading and literacy growth across the school, when I was struck by the question of whether teachers had the skills required to do the work we wanted them to do.

Had I and the school leadership team misdiagnosed our current "problem of practice," and should our focus be on improving teacher learning and building teaching expertise, in order to maximize student outcomes?

On returning to school and on further investigation, it became clear to me that this indeed was the place we needed to start. Our staff learning model was antiquated and ineffective. Professional learning was heavily reliant on external delivery and had no clear practical application or link to the classroom. Internal meetings were largely information delivery, and a number of staff regularly disengaged in school-led learning sessions.

There was also a lack of clarity amongst the teaching staff of the school's strategic intent: most had not read the Annual Implementation Plan (AIP), and many did not understand their role or responsibility in whole-school improvement.

Although there were "pockets of teaching excellence" across learning areas, teacher collaboration, a practical definition of what great teaching looked like in the classroom, and transparency in practice were not widespread. If we were going to achieve excellence in teaching and learning across the school, we needed to establish a professional learning community where everyone – teachers and leaders – accepted that they too were a learner, and that a core part of their work was to continue to improve their practice.

WHAT DID WE DO?

Over the last five years, our focus has been to revise staff learning and prioritize professional practice improvement. We have redesigned our meeting structure to be learning based, aligned to target "point of need" and connected to the current work. We have introduced a suite of professional learning structures as a way to personalize the learning offered by the school and provide greater ownership and autonomy to individual teachers. In addition, leadership learning walks, peer observation, a professional feedback model, and instructional coaching for teachers and leaders aim to de-privatize practice and make all our learning visible.

2017 – The Buddy Process: Building a Culture of Collaboration

We introduced the Design for Learning (D4L) pedagogical approach adopted by our entire school, in order to demystify our definition of what excellent practice looked like. Teachers were grouped into triads with a facilitator, who was not necessarily a member of the leadership team but a teacher who had confidence in the agreed pedagogy. Each teacher was asked to develop a learning

(Continued)

(Continued)

sequence, and then to collaborate with other teachers to refine the sequence further. It was clearly communicated that everyone was "in the sandpit" learning together, as not all the completed learning sequences would be taught. The focus was the process itself and understanding the specific pedagogical elements.

The process was incredibly successful, with teachers enjoying the opportunity to engage in pedagogical conversations with colleagues. There was an increased understanding of what the approach looked like, and the staff learning continuum evidenced significant growth in understanding across the staff.

The challenge at this stage was that, while a positive experience for most, this learning had been predominantly a planning process and had not yet challenged practice within the classroom. A number of teachers were also questioning the focus on staff learning and communicated a lack of certainty in the "why." A few, in Professional Development Plan (PDP) conversations, expressed apathy or actual reluctance regarding improving their practice at all, as it was clearly "good enough."

2018 – The Introduction of Professional Learning Teams: Learning Together

In the first semester of 2018, the school began the implementation of the D4L and the first learning sequences. To support this process, the buddy system was expanded to a Professional Learning Team (PLT) structure that emphasized collaboration. Teachers met weekly in year-level domain-based groups with a facilitator(s). All members of leadership were members of a PLT, and the Executive Team led professional learning as well as acted as a critical friend across the groups. Communication to staff emphasized that the purpose of this approach to staff learning was to maximize professional growth and improve *teaching*, not teachers.

Each PLT identified a "problem of practice" that they would work toward and would support the implementation of the D4L. In

DEVELOPING TEACHING EXPERTISE

addition, a database was developed to track focus areas and identify professional learning needs across the school, which was delivered predominantly by internal presenters.

The introduction of PLTs was, on one level, extremely successful. Most teachers found them a positive experience and enjoyed sharing their teaching experiences with others. Leadership noticed a change in language developing and that the focus of staff-room conversations had begun to shift from complaints regarding student behavior to discussions of learning strategies. Leadership learning walks also highlighted elements of the D4L being implemented in parts of the school, though this was still inconsistent.

The depth of conversations also varied amongst groups, with some demonstrating generative dialogue based on testing and trialing strategies in the classroom, while others could not even agree on a shared focus after weeks of debate, wanting to prioritize their own learning needs. We observed some "pockets of excellence" in teacher learning and other areas where theoretical discussion did not move to action in the classroom. Measuring the impact of PLTs on student learning growth was also challenging. Still, we had moved forward, and feedback at the end of the year confirmed we had achieved a common purpose, there was growing awareness of what was expected and a deeper understanding of what effective practice looked like, but not everyone was implementing that practice consistently in their classroom.

2019 – Ready, Fire, Aim and the Teaching Sprint

In 2019 my team and I began with a clear challenge. How would we move teachers from a place where they were comfortable in their learning to one where they experimented and took risks that expanded their current teaching practice? We knew this was critical if we were truly to improve practice.

(Continued)

(Continued)

How, too, would we ensure every staff member understood their role in whole school improvement and there were clearly established "through lines" between the school's strategic intent, the learning focus of PLTs, and what was happening in the classroom?

We needed a more structured approach. Each PLT still met weekly, but the facilitator's role was expanded to that of PLT leader, and each was responsible for implementing a framework for learning. This framework was designed to ensure the learning focus was evidence-informed, with an emphasis on being practical, targeted to point of teacher/student need, and with the clear intention of trialing the practices in classrooms.

Each team identified a Teaching Sprint (Breakspear & Ryrie-Jones, 2021), which took place during a semester. Teaching Sprints are short, sharp bursts of practice improvement that follow a three-part process: Prepare, Sprint, and Review (which included at least six weeks of deliberate practice in which teachers tried, tested, and experimented). This approach revolutionized our professional learning. PLTs moved from "talking about teaching" to "practicing their teaching" and monitoring their own progress.

The impact was immediate. Staff feedback was positive, and most welcomed the more structured framework. While fears surfaced again regarding leadership intent and purpose, immediately before we began the first round of observations, most found the opportunity to watch others enacting their sprint strategy a powerful learning experience.

A Teaching Sprint map that captured the areas of focus across the school demonstrated the high level of staff engagement and an increase in the quality of learning conversations. More teachers were taking a "leap of faith" and experimenting with new elements of practice, and some were beginning to embed these into their day-to-day teaching.

The year began positively, and we were poised to rapidly transition into key improvement work through the collaborative framework we had established.

And then suddenly the year turned into one no one expected. We, like everyone else in education, were scrambling to meet the challenge of an immediate move to remote learning. We were back in the "sand pit" as learners and had no choice but to take risks, trial, experiment, and accept permission to make mistakes. Despite the significant upheaval caused by teaching and working remotely for an extended period of time, the significant work we had put into developing teams that were able to adapt and respond put us in a strong position to deal with this educational challenge. PLTs continued to meet and collaborate during remote teaching and provided timely support through this period of significant change. The teams were so embedded as a way of working to deal with challenges that they found a way to continue despite teachers working from home. The reality is that incredible insights and learning took place in 2020, just not in the ways we anticipated at the beginning of the year.

My Leadership Learning

Building a culture in which teachers and leaders as well as students are recognized and valued as learners is incredibly challenging work that requires a shared purpose and utilization of momentum to maintain energy. As the principal and "lead learner," don't underestimate the impact of sharing your vulnerability or moments when you are in the learning pit too. Everyone makes mistakes.

For teacher learning to be powerful and to challenge existing mental models, the learning needs to be relevant to teachers' day-to-day work, accessible, safe, and engaging. Teachers need to understand the "Why" in order to invest the learning energy

(Continued)

(Continued)

required. The experience, whenever possible, should be "hands on" and biased toward action. Defining what excellent practice looks like is critical, so that everyone knows what they are working toward and what changes they need to make in their current practice.

Managing the balance between "teacher agency" in their own learning and the strategic direction of the school is also a challenge. Aiming to build collective autonomy, where individuals can see clear through-lines from the goals they are working toward in their classrooms and those in the AIP, builds shared responsibility for improvement and is critical to building excellent practice.

Gathering evidence of the direct impact of staff learning on student learning outcomes in the classroom is fundamental but incredibly complex. As a principal, I now understand that the measurement of improvements in a teacher's practice won't necessarily be evident in "big data" immediately, but it will be observable when you walk, watch, listen to stories, and collect staff and student feedback. There is incredible power in recording and capturing "learning stories."

ACTION ITEMS

In the interest of establishing adaptive teaching teams and collaborative expertise, it is important that school leaders not only consider how to enhance specific practices, but also carefully consider barriers that may inhibit collaborative ways of working. Following are two key actions that school leaders can take to support adaptive teaching teams and develop collaborative expertise:

- Intentionally counteract the human desire to socially loaf.

- Consciously lead with questions, not orders.

Counteract the Human Desire to Socially Loaf

There is no doubt that many of life's tasks can be better accomplished in groups. In our personal lives, when a task is quite big, such as catering for a child's birthday party, we might draw on friends and family to help us get the food organized. In this scenario, we would pool inputs from individuals (e.g., establish their "go to" recipe) to ensure that the overall success of the food on the day is a collective task. Everyone undertaking a smaller task supports the greater good.

However, as much as we might hate to admit, we have all been in a situation where we have not completed something as promised and unfortunately learned that it did not actually matter whether we contributed. When a group begins to work in this way, a few individuals might start going above and beyond the required task (e.g., bring more food) just in case some don't follow through with their commitment. Going above and beyond clearly originates from a good place but may only reinforce the notion that it is okay for some people in the group not to contribute. The end result is some individuals doing more than their share of work for the group, while others are "socially loafing."

Social loafing is a reduction in motivation and effort when individuals work collectively compared with when they work individually (Karau & Williams, 1993). Identifying the conditions under which individuals do or do not engage in social loafing is a complex issue, but Karau and Williams (1993) identified some clear reasons why social loafing may occur, such as decreased motivation when individuals perceive their efforts will not be recognized or when they feel their contribution is not necessary for the group to achieve high-quality outcomes. In some cases, people tend to match their effort with that of their co-workers and decide to lower their effort to maintain the equity of the group.

It is important to remember that social loafing shouldn't be used to judge the character of the people you are working with. They are neither bad nor lazy; they are human. Nevertheless, it is prudent to consider how to combat social loafing when establishing a collaborative environment. One strategy is to move from social loafing to social facilitation. Social facilitation is the concept that people will improve their task performance when they are in the presence of others as compared to being alone. The aim is to have teachers sharing and learning how to become more expert by developing the enabling conditions for authentic collaboration to occur. With this in mind, there are some specific ways teacher teams and leaders can consider countering social loafing and aiding shared mental models and collective expertise to flourish.

- *Develop shared direction.* In teams that possess shared direction, team members not only are clear about the goals and direction of the team, but also have been involved in establishing them. Decisions are made with an appropriate degree of debate and discussion. Shared direction combats a lack of coordination that can happen when there is ambiguity, and it helps teams self-organize and focus their efforts.

- *Establish individual agency.* Individual agency is about ensuring individual team members believe their role is important to the team. Determining how to make each member's role integral results in individuals not wanting to let the team down and exerting more effort to ensure the group performs highly. While it is important to focus on the positive interdependence of the group, it is essential to maintain individual agency. High-functioning teams create a dual purpose, in which an individual is responsible for contributing to the group while also being responsible for demonstrating his or her own learning.

- *Build low-level relational accountability.* Relational accountability can be established by ensuring each team member's contributions are defined and observable to the team. An individual's contributions might be *task oriented* (what they need to do) or *learning oriented* (what new knowledge or practices have resulted from the collaborative experience). If individuals have clarity around what is expected, and this is agreed by the group, they are more likely to follow through.

- *Promote reflective dialogue.* To promote learning, all members of the group will benefit from reflective dialogue and productive interactions. Developing clear protocols and processes for group discussions and decision-making will help the team develop clear ways of working.

Lead With Questions, Not Orders

Well-designed and well-facilitated professional conversations provide the means for collective learning through the development of shared meaning and the creation of new (contextualized) professional knowledge (Conway & Andrews, n.d.). School leaders should aim to grow their discussion and dialogue skills in areas such as listening and asking questions, sharing insights and feedback, reframing what has been discussed, and modeling reflective dialogue. They need to be critically aware of the way dialogue can shape team dynamics for the better or worse.

In fact, leadership is largely enacted through a series of discussions between a leader and a teacher (or a leader and a group of teachers). These discussions become critical in shaping the way teams work and how a psychologically safe culture is developed. Dialogue should be seen as one of the main mechanisms to build an environment of trust. Being cognizant of how to manage dialogue and use it as a tool to motivate, inspire, provoke further insight, or – perhaps – signal their own vulnerability is an important skill for school leaders to continually develop.

As Timperley (2015) noted, professional knowledge is constructed through social interaction and is situated and enacted in social communities of practice. Conversations are essential to its development (Orland-Barak, 2006). There is no doubt discussion might sometimes require a leader to "push" teachers (advising, modeling, and quite possibly confronting) while at times also "pulling" them (encouraging, supporting, and reassuring). This dynamic aspect of leadership will constantly ebb and flow, but it is critical to establishing an environment where adaptive teams can flourish.

Effective school leaders are deeply curious about the teachers and students they work with. Quality questioning techniques are a key mechanism used to delve into the thinking and actions of others. A good question can wedge open a door that might have remained closed. A good question can bring to the surface underlying assumptions, provoke insight, or compel a team to closely examine their motivations, aspirations, choices, and actions. The most useful questions can help teachers explore themselves and their motivations more deeply or challenge them to question their own perspectives and push themselves out of their comfort zone (Bacon & Voss, 2012). Consider using these key question types:

- *Situation questions*: Situation questions are used to gather facts about what is currently happening. These are important for drawing out information. *What practice is the team looking to explore? What does this currently look like in your classroom?*

- *Motivation questions*: Motivation questions are used to explore motivations, decision-making processes, and priorities. They can generate considerable insight about how the teachers are thinking and what is important to them. *Why do you see this practice as an important one to explore? How would this practice benefit our students?*

- *Ideal outcome questions*: Ideal outcome questions are about encouraging teachers to think about not only the future, but also what they see as an ideal future. These questions are best used when teachers are attempting to mobilize research into evidence-informed practices. *If there were no barriers, what could be possible with this practice? What would be the best possible outcome you see here?*

- *Clarifying questions*: Clarifying questions have two main purposes. The first is obviously to clarify something that has been said. The second is to exercise skepticism without appearing to be divisive. *How will that work? Why do you think approaching it in this way would be more effective than that way? Tell me more about [insert situation or problem].*

DISCUSSION QUESTIONS

- What are some barriers to meaningful collaboration, and how could you overcome these?

- Do teaching teams in your school have agreed norms for communication, evidence collection and analysis, and decision-making?

- How can you ensure teams still maintain a level of individual accountability?

- What are your strengths and aspirations to lead with questions and dialogue? Do you carefully consider the type of questions you ask?

CHAPTER 5

Understanding and Developing Teaching Dispositions

There has been a relatively recent shift in education toward focusing on the development of aptitudes and attitudes that will equip young people to function well under conditions of complexity, uncertainty, and individual responsibility – to help them become real-life learners (Carr & Claxton, 2002). There is a growing consensus that "learning to learn," as Burgogne (1998) described it, is the "ultimate life skill for the 21st century." However, when we scan the teacher professional learning literature, it is evident the impetus to develop teachers as lifelong learners does not appear to be embraced with the same fervor.

In fact, many professional learning structures for teachers follow a step-by-step process, and, although a process is important, it can't be the endgame. The emphasis on teachers working through a fixed process might be part of the reason we see so much variation in the impact of teacher learning. A lockstep process may actually stifle improvement, as the desire to check off each stage outweighs the impetus to learn and strive for deep insights. Completing a process creates a feeling of accomplishment, but sometimes no actual learning has taken place.

With this in mind, school leaders should consider what it means to help the teachers they work with to develop lifelong learning dispositions and self-evaluative capabilities. In other words, it is important to consider processes that support teachers in *how* to learn, so that they can make sense about *what* is suitable for their context and capabilities at any particular time.

RESEARCH EVIDENCE

Veenman (2008) illustrated that learning strategies can be more important than raw smarts when it comes to gaining expertise. So, considering how teachers learn is critical, it is a notion that is often underexplored in the research literature on teacher professional learning. The connection between an expertise pathway (the *what*) and the professional learning structure (the *how*) is important to consider, and striving for a balance between the two is a tightrope that educational leaders must constantly walk.

When it comes to learning something new, people who closely monitor and evaluate their thinking will outscore those who have high IQ levels (Veenman, 2008). Leaders need to help teachers become fluent in improvement techniques (peer coaching, learning walks, lesson study, etc.) while, at the same time, cultivating evaluative competencies to develop their expertise.

Carr and Claxton (2002) explored some key considerations when conceptualizing what it means to develop learning capabilities:

> Capabilities are the skills, strategies, and abilities which learning requires; what you might think of as the "toolkit" for learning. To be a good learner, you have to be able. But if such capabilities are necessary, they are not themselves sufficient. One has to be disposed to learn, ready and willing to take learning opportunities. (p. 10)

Though the word "disposition" can be quite ambiguous, it points very usefully at a domain of human attributes that are clearly different from "knowledge, skill, and understanding" (Carr & Claxton, 2002). Perkins et al. (1993) argued that a disposition has three aspects: skill, inclination, and sensitivity to occasion. They suggested that to be disposed to act in a certain way involves being competent to do so and being aware of when it is appropriate to do so.

Lucas and Nacer (2015) used the example of hand-washing among health-care professionals in hospitals to illustrate the interrelationship between knowledge, skills, and dispositions. In terms of knowledge, most health-care professionals understand the basic science of sanitizing hands to reduce the spread of infection. This knowledge has been commonplace since Semmelweis advocated for it over 100 years ago, and it certainly became even more important during the COVID-19 pandemic. In terms of difficulty, cleaning one's hands effectively is a relatively simple skill to acquire. Yet while individuals might possess knowledge and the skill of hand-washing, this may not lead to any change in behavior. To achieve change, knowledge and skill need to become routine habits of action (Lucas & Nacer, 2015). It is those habits, linked with skills and knowledge, that lead to a disposition of cleanliness.

Similarly, teachers might have the knowledge and skill to undertake a task, but they also need a habitual inclination to the task if an improvement process is to work to its fullest potential. As Perkins et al. (1993) noted, there needs to be some sort of "sensitivity to occasion." In other words, you act on the disposition by being sensitive to opportunities, able to engage in opportunities, and inclined toward opportunities.

As Carr and Claxton (2002) pointed out, the two aspects of being *able* and being *disposed* interact. That is, developing ability fosters success, and success tends to make a person more inclined to engage in the successful activity. As such, the disposition to learn leads to greater engagement and thus to the development of greater ability. But they also pointed out that the relationship is an uncertain one: capability does not always produce disposition, and disposition does not always produce capability (Carr & Claxton, 2002). This highlights the notion that skills and knowledge are still, and will always remain, vitally important for teachers. However, school leaders need to consider and cultivate the dispositions that promote meaningful learning experiences for teachers.

> Developing ability fosters success, and success tends to make a person more inclined to engage in the successful activity.

Although exploring learning dispositions might be new terrain for teacher professional learning, it is quite common among other professions. Industries such as engineering have well-articulated ways of thinking and acting so that they can develop important dispositions and competencies. Engineers are clear about not only what they do, but also how they think. Lucas et al. (2013) researched the dispositions of engineers and engineering educators and identified six habits related to engineering design processes: systems-thinking, problem-finding, visualizing, improving, creative problem-solving, and adaptability.

This is quite distinct from teacher professional learning, in which most models and structures are conceptualized with little or no reference to the habits and dispositions required to undertake the process in a meaningful way. Without the cultivation of these dispositions, the learning process is susceptible to becoming a lockstep, rigid one that may not lead to any improvement.

So, although teacher professional learning is discussed as a process with predetermined steps, it is also important to consider it as a way of thinking and acting. That is, it may require more than procedural skill and knowledge to engage in a professional learning process; it may also require key tenets of inquiry, such as being inquisitive and curious, to influence the way learners think and act. These complementary tenets of thinking and acting can be conceptualized as dispositions.

Within this paradigm, making teacher professional learning effective may require teachers to not only focus on improving their skills and knowledge, but also to consider altering their habits. Leaders should work to identify the underlying dispositions associated with preferred habits and then intentionally support teachers to develop these dispositions.

Crucial Dispositions for Teacher Professional Learning

Our recent research (Dunn, 2020, 2021; Dunn et al., 2019) explored the idea that a better understanding of teachers' learning dispositions could lead to a more precise understanding of the learning environment and processes that best cultivate the desired dispositions. That is, we sought to answer the following question: What are the dispositions that are particularly crucial for teacher professional learning, and how might we deliberately support teachers to develop these? The intention was to carefully identify and study the dispositions of teachers who engaged in a collaborative professional learning initiative. The discussion could then shift to how these dispositions can be cultivated in the design of professional learning programs for teachers.

The professional learning program we examined required teachers to explore research evidence, identify possible teaching practices, make decisions, and trial context-specific solutions. We identified the following behaviors of interest for our study: engaging with evidence, collaborating with colleagues, taking an action-oriented stance, undertaking continuous experimentation teaching cycles, seeking feedback, and gathering evidence to guide new iterations of the practice. The research sought to highlight the learning dispositions linked to these behaviors and whether they enhanced or constrained teachers' growth during the professional learning experience.

Each of the teachers who participated in the study reported on the specific characteristics of the professional learning experience he or she attributed to promoting or inhibiting development. In exploring the commonalities and differences between individuals as well as groups of teachers, four clear dispositions emerged.

Disposition 1: Collaborative

Teachers who reported the largest impact on their teaching practices from the professional learning initiative were those who recognized the value of other people's ideas and perspectives. These teachers continually referenced a collaborative mindset, in which sharing of ideas and working closely with other colleagues were seen as key aspects of the learning experience. They identified the importance of collaborating with teachers from schools that had similar contexts and circumstances to their own. The collaborative and supportive environment where teachers designed instructional solutions together pushed them to think more broadly and deeply about the instructional strategies they could trial in their classrooms.

Teachers also viewed collaboration as a motivating factor, in which the relational aspect of the program led them to be energized by one another. Just as they value their students being able to share and learn from one another on a daily basis, the professional learning gave teachers an authentic opportunity to share ideas with colleagues within their own school as well as with those from different schools.

Identifying the benefits of collaboration is not a particularly novel observation in education, and collegiality is a notion that has claimed to support school improvement for quite a while (Marzano, 2003). However, Fullan and Hargreaves (1996) cautioned that genuine collegiality cannot be contrived. Collegiality should be characterized by authentic interactions that are professional in nature (Marzano, 2003). These behaviors include openly sharing failures and mistakes, demonstrating respect for each other, and constructively analyzing and criticizing practices and procedures.

Teachers highlighted how the collaborative professional learning experience helped them see the larger picture of school-improvement work. It gave individual teachers meaningful insights into what other teachers were doing, how teachers at different grade levels taught the curriculum, and how schools and individuals were approaching the implementation of evidence-informed practices. The teachers also reported that the professional learning initiative had created an atmosphere of collaboration, acceptance, and perseverance, which is something they recognized as important to cultivate at their own schools to support teaching practice improvement.

Disposition 2: Innovative

A consistent theme for teachers who reported much growth in their teaching practices was an inclination to take calculated risks. These teachers understood and articulated that improvement efforts inherently involve a degree of risk as they work through new pedagogical practices. Hattie (2009) emphasized this idea when he discussed innovation occurring as a teacher deliberately introduces a method of teaching that is different (not necessarily new) from what he or she currently uses. Teachers with an innovative disposition mitigated risk by basing instructional decisions on evidence-informed practices, even if they were not certain the practice would be immediately successful. These teachers viewed implementing innovative approaches as an iterative process of constant refinement, evaluation, and adjustment.

Lucas and Nacer (2015) supported this idea when they highlighted that innovators are adept at taking reasonable risks; that is, improvement involves playing with possibilities and daring to be different while always grounding the work with research evidence to support the new direction. Innovators want to ensure that perceived value and safety are carefully weighed against any possible risks associated with the new idea they are seeking to explore. They have the mindset that not taking action can be a greater risk than taking action.

> Innovators have the mindset that not taking action can be a greater risk than taking action.

Hattie (2009) emphasized that the most critical attributes when pursuing innovation are heightened attention to its effects and identifying the problem that the intervention is meant to ameliorate. Innovators know how to recognize and define information relevant to their purpose; consider alternatives; decide what to do; do it; determine whether they are satisfied with the results; and, if they are not, revise their practice until they are successful. All the while, they are learning through the experience.

Innovative teachers seek feedback about the impact of the innovation. This seeking is specific to the problem and carefully checked for unintended consequences. Thus, the innovation brings increased attention to evaluating the merit of the intervention. So, the definition of the innovative disposition must also include an evaluative aspect. Having an innovative disposition is about more than just trying new (or different) instructional practices; it is also about considering the utility and impact this work has for the students it is intended to help.

Disposition 3: Resilient

Lucas and Nacer (2015) discussed "adaptation and the ability to bounce back from adverse events as core to improvement" (p. 14). Teachers in our study supported this claim when they identified that what fostered deep learning was a certain level of challenge, rather than ease. They displayed the ability to keep going despite the difficulties, and they accepted that practice improvement was going to be challenging. They exhibited a belief that they could work through the challenges if they persevered. When teachers who reported much growth as part of the professional learning initiative confronted inevitable problems, they committed to remaining positive about their work and continuing to learn. This was evident to us in comments from these teachers that centered on how challenging the learning had been but how optimistic they were about the long-term benefits for their teaching practice and, in turn, their students.

We came to consider this mindset a resilient disposition. The notion of resilience as a learning disposition is supported by Carr and Claxton (2002), who stated:

> One of the key learning dispositions must surely be the inclination to take on (at least some) learning challenges where the outcome is uncertain, to persist with learning despite temporary confusion or frustration and to recover from setbacks or failures and rededicate oneself to the learning task. (p. 14)

There is no doubt school improvement is messy – and, at times, confusing – but this might actually be an essential part of the process. D'Mello and Graesser (2012), who investigated links between emotions and learning for over a decade, found that confusion can be beneficial to learning, because it can cause learners to process the material more deeply in order to resolve their confusion.

The key indicators of resilience include "sticking with a difficult learning task; having a relatively high tolerance for frustration without getting upset; [and] being able to recover from setback or disappointment relatively quickly" (Carr & Claxton, 2002, p. 14). In our research, these aspects were evident in teachers' responses in which they acknowledged the professional learning activities had been a transformational experience that encouraged them to use new and improved practices despite their having experienced challenges and frustration. Self-evaluation and feedback loops were also essential elements of the resilient disposition, as teachers described learning from their missteps and knowing that they would teach differently as a result of the learning.

Disposition 4: Curious

In our study, a curiosity toward learning and continual improvement in teaching practice was another hallmark of the teachers who reported the most growth. This seems logical, as curiosity is often seen as central to improvement. Beswick (2000) highlighted that curiosity does more than spur interest; it also links to perseverance:

> Highly curious people will remain longer than others in situations of uncertainty . . . they will have developed a range of investigative skills to help resolve conceptual conflicts by gathering additional information . . . they will have a sense of security in their world to put their cognitive map in jeopardy without debilitating anxiety, to run the risk of creating a new and better order, and they have the capacity to carry out the integration required to . . . create, maintain, and resolve conceptual conflicts. (p. 151)

Claxton et al. (2015) claimed that "curiosity is at the heart of all learning" (p. 157). Curious learners are inclined to know more, especially about novel or strange things (Beswick, 2000). An example of this comes from a fourth-grade teacher in our study who stated:

> It is a completely new and exciting experience for learning. The attitude in which my students come into my classroom is completely opposite to what it was at the beginning of the year. I come to work and enjoy the challenge of what is new and still unknown and leave each day with a smile.

Daniel Willingham (2014) explored the idea of making students more curious. He outlined how recent research shows that curiosity is related to academic performance. In fact, the combination of curiosity and conscientiousness – a feeling of responsibility to get things done – has as big an impact on grades as intelligence (Von Stumm et al., 2011). Willingham (2014) also noted that the definition of "curiosity" is general and usually varies widely, depending on the topic. He elaborated to suggest that we can be curious about any topic, and, conversely, topics we imagine would interest us may not actually spark our curiosity, depending on how we encounter them. This is critically important, because a teacher may be highly curious about practices related to literacy but be less so when exploring practices related to mathematics, or vice versa. Curiosity is not a permanent state and will relate strongly to what is being explored.

A person with a curious disposition has an orientation to delve into the experience of learning new skills and developing expertise. Because teacher professional learning usually begins with the assumption that existing practices can at least be improved (Edelson, 2006), curiosity appears to be a disposition that enhances the impact of teacher learning. In our research (Dunn, 2021), curiosity helped teachers carefully explore different iterations of practices in their school settings and work toward constructing increasingly practical and effective solutions. In a way, the disposition might be more accurately described as "critically curious," as there is a sense of analysis and reasoning to complement the curiosity. These teachers also articulated the importance of slowing down and deeply exploring practices, which enabled them to analyze what they were doing and establish clear next steps.

PRINCIPLES AND PRACTICES
How to Develop Teaching Dispositions Using Design

Although design may not be widely recognized as a central activity of teaching, designing evidence-informed interventions to meet context-specific needs is becoming a more universally expected way teachers should work. Teachers are increasingly asked to work through design processes that enable them to consider problems of practice, seek and utilize evidence to pursue solutions, and then implement the possible solutions in their classrooms. Design should now be at the heart of how teachers improve their practice and cultivate positive dispositions. In examining professions such as engineering, school leaders can learn how they have articulated ways of thinking and acting that support the development of desired habits, competencies, and dispositions.

For example, professions that are focused on design emphasize dispositions that prioritize problem-solving, learning from failure, innovation, teamwork, iterative testing of possible solutions, and critical analysis. For education to foster similar dispositions, teachers need to articulate the way they think and act when undertaking professional learning processes that require them to design, deliver, and reflect on evidence-informed, classroom-level interventions.

At the heart of this approach is the notion that by designing and carrying out focused, incremental learning cycles that investigate the impact of instructional practices, teachers will be able to continually grow their teaching expertise. While design approaches take many different forms, most design cycles follow a similar process: recognize and define information and research relevant to the purpose; consider alternatives; decide what to do; do it; determine whether the results are satisfactory; and, if they are not, revise the approach. All throughout this process, participants are learning through the experience. For teachers, they can become more responsive to their students' needs based on the evidence of what is (or is not) working in their classroom. Thus, embedding design processes in professional learning initiatives for teachers can support the development of desired dispositions, such as the collaborative, innovative, resilient, and curious ones discussed above.

To develop positive dispositions through teacher professional learning that is underpinned by the way designers think, there are some essential principles and practices school leaders need to consider:

- *Professional learning as a process.* For teachers to reap the benefits of professional learning, there needs to be a specific process to support the development of teaching expertise. Examples of professional learning processes are Teaching Sprints, Lesson Study, and Action Research (for more examples, see Chapter 1). No matter the type, professional learning processes that support expertise development usually follow a cycle – one that moves from identifying the problem, to designing and building a solution, to implementing and scaling the solution (Figure 5.1). The structure and purpose of a professional learning process is vitally important for teachers to effectively examine their teaching practices. A well-resourced process will give teachers the space and time to be able to do the work.

FIGURE 5.1   The Professional Learning Process

Identify the
problem

Design and build
a solution

Implement and
scale the solution

DEVELOPING TEACHING EXPERTISE

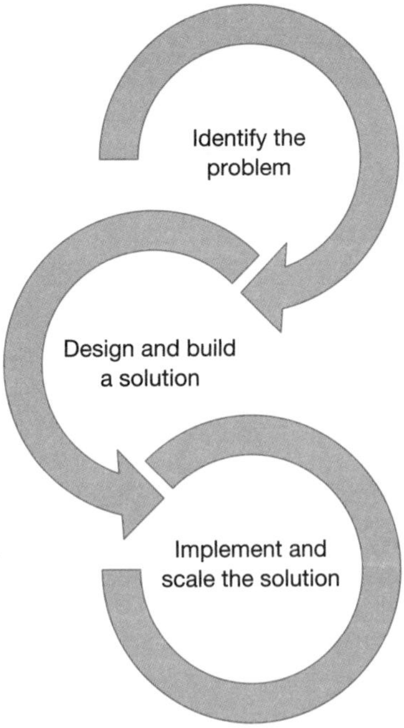

- *Professional learning as a way of working.* School leaders need to be able to justify why this way of working is beneficial to teachers and the students they teach. Leaders should position professional learning as an ongoing solution that teachers can utilize to collaboratively problem-solve around identified practice issues. In this way, teacher professional learning becomes more than a process and evolves into an embedded way the school addresses adaptive challenges that arise. Just like recreational golfers who periodically go to the driving range to improve their swing, teachers should see the benefits of embedding their own learning into how they work.

- *Professional learning as a way of thinking.* Professional learning is a way for educators to organize their thought processes around areas of focus. In essence, professional learning is a form of solution-focused thinking and acting. It should have similarities to the cognitive activities that designers apply during the process of designing. Designers employ strategies such as synthesis, divergent thinking, analysis, and convergent thinking in order to arrive at solutions. The thinking that results from the process is a key outcome for school leaders to seek.

STORY FROM THE FIELD

Lessons Learned From a District-Wide Professional Learning Intervention

▶ Supporting teachers to cultivate not only skills and knowledge, but also dispositions, entails significant challenges to how we conceptualize teacher learning and the key outcomes we seek. An approach that emphasizes the development of dispositions, knowledge, and skills aligns with arguments made by, for example, Biesta (2007), who emphasized the primacy of teachers, as professionals, to make the best decisions about what happens in their classrooms. Different classrooms require different, context-specific solutions.

(Continued)

(Continued)

FIGURE 5.2 Typology of a Teacher's Inquiry Disposition

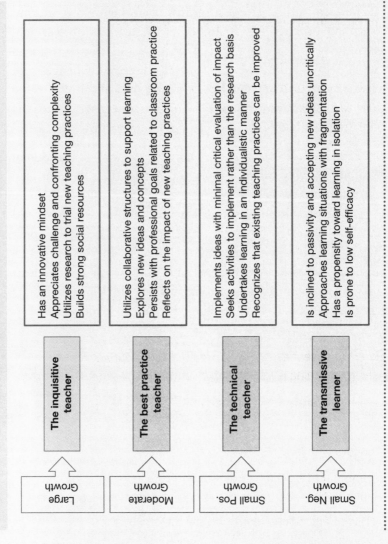

Large Growth	The inquisitive teacher	Has an innovative mindset Appreciates challenge and confronting complexity Utilizes research to trial new teaching practices Builds strong social resources
Moderate Growth	The best practice teacher	Utilizes collaborative structures to support learning Explores new ideas and concepts Persists with professional goals related to classroom practice Reflects on the impact of new teaching practices
Small Pos. Growth	The technical teacher	Implements ideas with minimal critical evaluation of impact Seeks activities to implement rather than the research basis Undertakes learning in an individualistic manner Recognizes that existing teaching practices can be improved
Small Neg. Growth	The transmissive learner	Is inclined to passivity and accepting new ideas uncritically Approaches learning situations with fragmentation Has a propensity toward learning in isolation Is prone to low self-efficacy

While previously in this chapter we have discussed the four key dispositions that emerged from our research (Dunn, 2020; Dunn et al., 2019), further analysis illustrated important differences between the individual teachers who participated in the study. More specifically, the comparative analysis revealed a typology with four types of teachers who participated in the professional learning initiative (Figure 5.2).

It is worth noting the four dispositions discussed in this chapter (collaborative, innovative, resilient, and curious) were prominently displayed by teachers who reported moderate to extensive growth as a result of the professional learning initiative. What became clear is that supporting teachers to develop the key characteristics of inquisitive teachers provides a useful framework for also developing the identified dispositions.

With that in mind, it will be prudent for you to explore the key characteristics of inquisitive teachers and consider how you could cultivate these with teachers in your school. Inquisitive teachers are keen to get beneath the surface – they are the opposite of passive. They are interested in questioning, critically thinking, and developing social resources, as well as making connections between research and practice. They are less likely than most people to accept information uncritically without knowing the reasoning behind it. They typically:

- display an innovative mindset that commits to continually stretching their teaching practice,
- appreciate challenge and confronting complexity,
- utilize research evidence to support trialing new teaching practices,
- seek to make connections and integrate ideas,
- build strong social resources by collaborating with colleagues within and outside of their school,
- are willing to wrestle with difficult concepts, and
- exhibit agency and take responsibility.

ACTION ITEMS

As discussed previously, one of the main issues with professional learning is that it is often defined, planned, and implemented as a process to undertake. While the process is certainly important, we also need to identify the specific habits teachers can enact that will enhance the impact of any professional learning process. A dual lens, one that focuses on the process as well as disposition development, is necessary. In this way, teacher professional learning is about developing teaching expertise by creating new habits of excellence over time and supporting teachers to sustain those habits.

Based on the research outlined in this chapter, there were some clear dispositions and attributes associated with teachers who reported a good deal of growth as a result of their professional learning experience. We categorized the teachers who were collaborative, innovative, resilient, and curious as "inquisitive teachers." These teachers were eager to get beneath the surface; they are the opposite of passive. They are interested in questioning, thinking critically, developing social resources, and making connections between research and practice. Inquisitive teachers are less likely than other teachers to accept information without being given the reasoning behind it. Inquisitive teachers typically exhibit the characteristics listed in this chapter.

It is important for school leaders to consider what they can do to contribute to teachers' maximal engagement in professional learning. The cultivation of dispositions that would lead to "inquisitive teachers" needs to be part of this conversation. What follows are actions leaders can take to influence the development of desired dispositions in their teaching staff.

Model the Dispositions You Seek From Others

As you seek to develop teachers' capabilities and dispositions, it is essential that you consider how to encourage teachers to be more curious and inquisitive about their practice. A good way to do this is to model the habits and dispositions you are seeking to cultivate. Inquisitive teachers are more likely to proliferate under inquisitive leaders.

As outlined in Chapter 3, a particularly effective way to model curiosity and an inquisitive nature is to ask lots of questions. Asking questions is likely to encourage teachers to voice their ideas and to seek diverse perspectives. We recommend leaders actively solicit dissenting views and do not shut down out-of-the-box ideas. When teachers feel that school leaders want to hear from them and value their perspectives, they will be more likely to have valuable input into discussions. They will also be more likely to develop the habits that lead to a desired disposition over time.

Build a Culture That Allows Desired Dispositions to Flourish

Google's 2015 study Project Aristotle found that psychological safety was the most significant success factor underpinning high-performance teams across the organization. Amy Edmondson (1999), of Harvard Business School, defined psychological safety as a belief that you will not be punished or humiliated for speaking up about ideas, questions, concerns, or errors. If we seek innovation that leads to improvement, then it is important that team members feel safe to make mistakes, ask questions, discuss difficult issues, and take risks. Leaders can create environments for learning where positive dispositions can flourish by acting in ways that promote psychological safety. Edmondson (2012) identified key leadership behaviors for developing psychological safety:

- *Be accessible and approachable.* Leaders can encourage team members to learn together by being accessible and personally involved.

- *Acknowledge the limits of current knowledge.* When leaders admit that they don't know something, their genuine display of humility will encourage other team members to follow suit.

- *Be willing to display fallibility.* To create psychological safety, team leaders must demonstrate a tolerance of failure by acknowledging their own missteps.

- *Invite participation.* When people believe their leaders value their input, they will be more engaged and responsive.

- *Highlight failures as learning opportunities.* Instead of punishing people for well-intentioned efforts that backfire, leaders should encourage team members to embrace error and deal with failure in a productive manner.

- *Use direct language.* Using direct, actionable language will instigate the type of straightforward discussion that enables learning.

- *Set boundaries.* When leaders are as clear as possible about what is acceptable, people will feel more psychologically safe than when boundaries are vague or unpredictable.

- *Hold people accountable for transgressions.* When people cross predetermined boundaries and fail to perform to standards, leaders must hold them accountable in a fair and consistent way.

DISCUSSION QUESTIONS

- In addition to fostering skills and knowledge, do you also consider habits, competencies, and dispositions when leading teacher professional learning? If not, how could you integrate these elements more intentionally?

- What role do you believe your school's culture plays in developing positive teacher dispositions? How might you influence that culture to be more conducive to the dispositions you'd like to see among your teachers?

Conclusion

Professional learning opportunities are designed for a variety of purposes. Regardless of the objectives of a given program, program administrators can often jump to measuring what is easiest and most obvious: participants' satisfaction with their immediate experience in the workshop, institute, or other program (Reeves, 2012). What is overlooked in this approach is the extent to which the program's aims have been met; the extent to which the participants were impacted by the professional learning experience; and, most importantly, how their teaching changed over time as a result of their experience and how their students' learning was affected (Guskey, 2002; Loucks-Horsley et al., 1998).

Increasingly, system leaders believe that "ambitious reforms cannot be developed at the drawing tables in government offices but call for systematic research supporting the development and implementation processes in a variety of contexts" (Plomp, 2007, p. 9). As such, the ability of schools to adjust evidence-informed practices in their contexts becomes critically important for educational leaders. In this context, the goal of school improvement and teacher professional learning is to support reform by enabling teachers to "test their effectiveness and search for new practices wherever they could be found in research and innovation" (Hargreaves & Fullan, 2012, p. 50).

Ensuring that there is agency over learning at a local level is important, as Glickman et al. (2004) identified that the nature of education demands that teachers be autonomous and flexible thinkers. If we fall short in this area, the alternative for teachers who are not supported to acquire the ability to "think abstractly and autonomously is to simplify and deaden the instructional environment" (Glickman et al., 2004, p. 69). This highlights the importance of deeply considering the way professional learning is often portrayed in dichotomous terms – "top down" versus "bottom up." This dichotomy is too simplistic; modern teacher professional learning and current policy requires an approach that can nurture both top-down and bottom-up improvement simultaneously. We ask you to consider and discuss: Does your professional learning framework strive for a balance between individual teachers' learning needs and whole-school direction?

As we stated in the preface, some experts have viewed the impact of professional learning as low. Opfer and Pedder (2011) noted that, in England, "professional development of teachers . . . is generally ineffectual and lacks school level systems and supports" and that the association between performance management and teacher professional learning in low-performing schools is particularly problematic. Guskey (2002) remarked that, in the United States, reviews of professional-development research consistently point out the ineffectiveness of most programs. This, Guskey argued, is in part due to forced compliance in professional-development programs and thus lower motivation to engage. The professional learning programs too often fail to appreciate that teachers walk into the room already with strong theories of how they teach, which are often not taken into account.

However, the world of professional learning continues; there are so many options, so many presenters, so many views about the pros and cons. According to the twenty-three meta-analyses (analyzing over one thousand studies, which include

6 million students) on the impact of teacher professional learning, the average effect size on student achievement is 0.37, but with marked variation (from 0.10 to 0.80). Clearly, there are high-impact professional-development practices that enhance the learning lives of students. This book has sought to highlight the underlying picture of successful professional learning, and it very much comes back to investing in the evaluative thinking of educators, as well as ensuring commitment of time, resources, and expertise to collaboratively focus efforts to maximize the impact of educators.

This focus on evaluative thinking highlights that the major concern of professional development is enhancing educators' expertise. Such attention to the attributes of expert teachers (in terms of those who have the greatest positive impact on students) can help us diagnose what is needed in professional learning and help us identify what is meant by adaptive teaching expertise. A key concept is that expert teachers know the limits of their knowledge and are able to seek help; they continually learn and collaborate with others in diagnosing, problem-solving, and evaluating the impact of the chosen solutions. It helps when professional learning is conducted collaboratively within and across schools (with the principals present and participating). Any professional-development program's success depends on transparency – regarding not only its purpose, but also the fact that the professional learning is being evaluated during (and not only after) the program. The "so what" question about merit, worth, and significance is critical to the credibility, the motivation, and thus the impact of participating in the learning.

> Expert teachers continually learn and collaborate with others in diagnosing, problem-solving, and evaluating the impact of the chosen solutions.

Time is also an important consideration. For teachers to effectively self-monitor and undertake meaningful professional learning, they need sufficient time. As Timperley et al. (2007) concluded, "Extended timeframes and frequent contact were probably necessary because . . . the process of changing teaching practice involved substantive new learning that, at times, challenged existing beliefs, values, and/or the understandings that underpinned that practice" (p. xxviii). Although time allocation is complicated, we know that if there is insufficient time, teachers may feel pressured to pursue short-term goals that revolve around finding what Appleton (2006) described as "activities that work." This is where teachers are given activities to do in their classrooms without exploring, or understanding, the pedagogy and content that underpins the learning experience.

We outlined how adaptive school leaders can increase the impact of teacher learning, such as by:

- developing a mindset of acceptance of continuous improvement;

- empowering teachers to respond to their unique context;

- developing an implementation action model;

- focusing on teams, not individuals;

- designing lean improvement processes; and

- fostering psychological safety.

As a school leader, you need to be proficient in evaluating the fidelity, adaptations, dosage, and quality of the professional learning that is taking place. Developing this capability will help you not only know when to discontinue programs that have too little effect relative to their cost and effort, but also highlight and celebrate the collective impact of your staff when there is success. Evaluative leaders will continually ask questions such as these:

- How do we know this is working?

- How can we compare this practice with that one?

- Where is the evidence that shows that this is superior to other options?

- What evidence would I accept that it is not working (or not working as well as intended)?

- What is the magnitude of this improvement work?

- Where have we seen this practice implemented so that it produces effective results?

As noted in Chapter 3, evaluative school leaders are able to identify key areas of focus for improvement, be deliberate and intentional with implementation, be problem-solvers and hypothesis-testers, be cognizant of their impact on teachers, and actively seek second opinions.

An underexplored area in the professional learning literature is the support needed for teachers to navigate the dual role of teacher and learner. We know issues can arise, as continued job-embedded learning requires a set of skills, dispositions, and a way of working that may be unfamiliar to a classroom practitioner. One fundamental issue that is often associated with professional learning is the inevitable, albeit unintended, bias that can occur when teachers inquire into their own practice. An important way of tempering this bias is to have teachers work within a collaborative environment, so that assumptions can be challenged and evidence is interrogated.

The collective nature of improvement work leads to the continued debate about collective efficacy – the joint belief of all adults in the school of their ability to positively impact all students, have high expectations for all, and have the skills and confidence to work together on this mission. Despite the evidence to support collective efficacy, we are beginning to see that many efforts focused on improving it have had little effect. The key reason for this is that unless there is a clear focus on the impact to students, it is difficult to realize the power of collective efficacy. Collective efficacy is about ensuring that any improvement initiative is underpinned by rigorous diagnosis of the current situation, implementation and monitoring of new or evolved practices, and questioning and seeking evidence about whether the gains are sufficient. Unless progress is visible, it will be difficult to cultivate collective efficacy. Unless improvement is viewed with an evaluative mindset, it will be difficult to establish progress.

Undertaking this work within a collaborative framework increases the likelihood that teachers will work together to solve issues that arise and provides a built-in mechanism for scaling improved practices across the school. This entails empowering teaching teams to focus on student learning, promoting reflective dialogue and productive interactions, cultivating positive interdependence between teachers while retaining individual accountability, and monitoring implementation and being responsive to emerging evidence.

According to Schön (1983, 1987), teachers develop professional knowledge through a process of defining and solving problems. Goodson (1997, pp. 19–20) viewed the best way for teachers to improve their practice as researching and reflecting upon their own practice. Thus, "great teachers" all "constantly reflect upon and refine their practice, try new things, work at what is not working well and think through the problems that face them" (Maaranen, 2009, p. 220). These are all essential components of effective teacher learning.

Although Goodson (1997) did not state so directly, students' needs should be considered at the forefront of the improvement process. Teachers should examine the impact they are having on their students and use this focus in a continuous cycle of practice improvement. The inherent risk is that teachers who miss this key factor may move toward what works better for *them* (even on a subconscious level), rather than the students they teach. From our research (Dunn, 2020; Dunn et al., 2019), we know that educators who best achieve these ends possess skills of collaboration, a disposition to embrace innovation, resilience to try and try again to impact on all students, and a genuine curiosity as to how they can improve. The question is – is this normal practice in your school?

Glossary

Adaptive mindset is both an intellectual stance that creates the preconditions for being adaptive and a particular pattern of decision-making in complex situations (Grisogono & Radenovic, 2007). It is a mindset that treats improvement as the beginning of an iterative process of testing a hypothesis, observing what happens, learning, making course corrections, and then, if necessary, trying something else (Heifetz et al., 2009).

Adaptive teams have a relentless focus on improving teaching practice and responding to the needs of the students they teach. Teachers working in a supportive way to help each other improve, analyze student learning, plan, and problem solve is a worthwhile goal to pursue.

Collaborative expertise is individually held knowledge structures that help team members function in a team environment (McComb & Simpson, 2014). It has been established in teamwork studies that team mental models improve teams' ability to communicate and coordinate (Converse et al., 1993).

Collective efficacy is a group's shared belief in its conjoint capability to organize and execute the courses of action required to produce given levels of attainment (Bandura, 1997).

Design processes are a series of steps aimed at designing a practice in order to solve a problem. Design processes involve envisioning, designing, building, and testing the solution.

Enabling conditions are situations that must occur simultaneously with a given initiating event to support improvement. They include school culture, mindsets, and structures for improvement.

Evaluative thinking is a systematic reflective process that manifests as questioning, seeking evidence, and learning in order to establish an informed position; it involves a clear chain of reasoning that connects data to a grounded conclusion (Schwandt, 2008).

Evidence of impact identifies the consequences of our actions and the extent to which program or project goals have been achieved. Evidence of impact is underpinned by being clear about improvement objectives, identifying improvement, and seeking to explain change that is occurring.

Expertise pathways are precise specifications of practice that are defined in a sequential manner as your expertise develops within an area. They provide a map of how teachers can become increasingly adept within specific areas of practice.

Feedback loop is a cause-effect process in which output data are recycled as input; it is a sequence or process that uses outcomes to inform subsequent decisions and operations.

Formative evaluation is an evidence-collection process designed to identify potential and actual influences on the progress and effectiveness of implementation efforts. Formative evaluation enables teachers and school leaders to explicitly study the complexity of implementation programs and identify ways to answer questions about context, adaptations, and response to change.

Instructional rounds involve a group of leaders and/or teachers visiting multiple classrooms in their school, with the aim of identifying teaching and learning trends that are occurring. Instructional rounds should be ongoing, structured classroom visits intended to gather data about teaching and learning through observation and interaction with students. The trends identified are to be used as a basis to support a wider discussion on teaching and learning within the school.

Learning walks involve a group of leaders and teachers visiting multiple classrooms in their own or another school to observe exemplary practice. The observation needs to be focused on a specific area, with the aim of spreading that practice and supporting the scaling of systemic improvements of teaching and learning across the school.

Summative evaluation evidence evaluates, at the end of an implementation strategy, whether that strategy has led to improvement. This is achieved by comparing it against an established standard or benchmark.

Teacher inquiry can be collaborative and is about developing new and relevant local knowledge. It encourages teachers to be collaborators in revising curriculum, improving their work environment and teaching practices, professionalizing teaching, and developing policy.

Team mental models are knowledge structures that allow team members to understand and form expectations about how a system operates (Rouse et al., 1992; Rouse & Morris, 1986); they enable team members to establish criteria for each other's responsibilities, needs, and behaviors (Mohammed et al., 2000).

Bibliography

Amabile, T., & Kramer, S. (2011). *The progress principle: Using small wins to ignite joy, engagement, and creativity at work*. Harvard Business Review Press.

Appleton, K. (2006). Science pedagogical content knowledge and elementary school teachers. In K. Appleton (Ed.), *Elementary science teacher education: International perspectives on contemporary issues and practice* (pp. 31–54). Lawrence Erlbaum in association with the Association for Science Teacher Education.

Australian Curriculum, Assessment and Reporting Authority. (2014). *Foundation to Year10 Curriculum*.

Australian Curriculum, Assessment and Reporting Authority. (2018). *The Australian Curriculum*. Australian Curriculum and Reporting Authority. http://www.australiancurriculum.edu.au

Australian Institute for Teaching and School Leadership. (2017). *How to guide – peer observation*.

Axelrod, R., & Cohen, M. D. (2000). *Harnessing complexity: Organizational implications of a scientific frontier*. Basic Books.

Bacon, T. R., & Voss, L. (2012). *Adaptive coaching: The art and practice of a client-centered approach to performance improvement* (2nd ed.). Nicholas Brealy Publishing.

Bandura, A. (1997). *Self-efficacy: The exercise of control*. W. H. Freeman and Company.

Berliner, D. C. (1991). Educational psychology and pedagogical expertise: New findings and new opportunities for thinking about training. *Educational Psychologist, 26*(2), 145–155.

Berliner, D. C. (2001). Learning about and learning from expert teachers. *International Journal of Educational Research, 35*(5), 463–482.

Berliner, D. C. (2004). Describing the behavior and documenting the accomplishments of expert teachers. *Bulletin of Science, Technology & Society, 24*(3), 200–212.

Berry, A. (2020). Disrupting to driving: Exploring upper primary teachers' perspectives on student engagement. *Teachers and Teaching: Theory and Practice, 26*(2), 1–21.

Beswick, D. (2000). *An introduction to the study of curiosity*. Melbourne, Australia: Centre for Applied Educational Research, University of Melbourne. http://www.beswick.info/psychres/curiosityintro.htm

Biesta, G. (2007). Why "what works" won't work: Evidence-based practice and the democratic deficit in educational research. *Educational Theory, 57*(1), 1–22.

Boaler, J. (2008a). Promoting "relational equity" and high mathematics achievement through an innovative mixed-ability approach. *British Educational Research Journal, 34*(2), 167–194. doi:10.1080/01411920701532145

Boaler, J. (2008b). *What's math got to do with it? Helping children learn to love their most hated subject – and why it's important for America.* Penguin.

Borko, H. (2004). Professional development and teacher learning: Mapping the terrain. *Educational Researcher, 33*(8), 3–15.

Breakspear, S., & Ryrie-Jones, B. (2021). *Teaching Sprints: How overloaded educators can keep getting better.* Corwin.

Brookfield, S. (2003). Putting the critical back in critical pedagogy: A commentary on the path of dissent. *Journal of Transformative Education, 1,* 141–149.

Burgogne, J. (1998). A declaration on learning. *People Management, 1,* 28–29.

Carr, M., & Claxton, G. (2002). Tracking the development of learning dispositions. *Assessment in Education: Principles, Policy & Practice, 9*(1), 9–37.

Centre for Educational Statistics and Evaluation. (2015). *Evaluative thinking.* https://education.nsw.gov.au/teaching-and-learning/professional-learning/pl-resources/evaluation-resource-hub/evaluative-thinking

Chen, G., Sharma, P. N., Edinger, S. K., Shapiro, D. L., & Farh, J. L. (2011). Motivating and demotivating forces in teams: Cross-level influences of empowering leadership and relationship conflict. *Journal of Applied Psychology, 96*(3), 541–557.

City, E. A., Elmore, R. F., Fiarman, S. E., & Teitel, L. (2009). *Instructional rounds in education: A network approach to improving teaching and learning.* Harvard Education Press.

Claxton, G., Lucas, B., Byron, T., & Black, O. (2015). *Educating Ruby: What our children really need to learn.* Crown House Publishing.

Cochran-Smith, M., & Lytle, S. L. (1999). Relationships of knowledge and practice: Teacher learning in communities. *Review of Research in Education, 24,* 249–305.

Common Core State Standards Initiative. (2011). *Common core state standards for mathematics.*

Converse, S., Cannon-Bowers, J. A., & Salas, E. (1993). Shared mental models in expert team decision making. In N. J. Castellan, Jr. (Ed.), *Individual and group decision making: Current issues* (pp. 221–246). Lawrence Erlbaum Associates, Inc.

Conway, A., & Andrews, D. (n.d.). *Time to talk: The LRI handbook for facilitating professional conversation.* Leadership Research International, University of Southern Queensland. https://lri.usq.edu .au/our-research/publications

Cooper, A. (2010, May 1). *Knowledge brokers: A promising knowledge mobilization strategy to increase research use in education.* Paper presented at the annual meeting of the American Educational Research Association, Denver, CO, United States.

Coovert, M. D., Craiger, J. P., & Cannon-Bowers, J. A. (1996). Innovations in modeling and simulating team performance: Implications for decision making. In R. A. Guzzo & E. Salas (Eds.), *Team effectiveness and decision making in organizations* (pp. 149–203). Jossey-Bass.

Cordingley, P. (2015). The contribution of research to teachers' professional learning and development. *Oxford Review of Education, 41*(2), 234–252.

Davidoff, F., Dixon-Woods, M., Leviton, L., & Michie, S. (2015). Demystifying theory and its use in improvement. *BMJ Quality & Safety, 24*(3), 228–238. doi:10.1136/bmjqs-2014-003627

Deans for Impact. (2016). *Practice with purpose: The emerging science of teacher expertise.* https://deansforimpact.org/wp-content/uploads/ 2016/12/Practice-with-Purpose_FOR-PRINT_113016.pdf

Desimone, L. (2009). Improving impact studies of teachers' professional development: Towards better conceptualizations and measures. *Educational Researcher, 38*(3), 181–199.

D'Mello, S., & Graesser, A. (2012). Dynamics of affective states during complex learning. *Learning and Instruction, 22*(2), 145–157.

Doecke, B., Parr, G., & North, S. (2008). *National mapping of teacher professional learning project.* Faculty of Education, Monash University.

Dunn, R. (2011). *Engaging in practitioner based action research to develop an individualised professional learning model* [unpublished master's thesis]. Monash University.

Dunn, R. (2020). Adaptive leadership: Leading through complexity. *International Studies in Educational Administration (Commonwealth Council for Educational Administration & Management (CCEAM)), 48*(1).

Dunn, R. (2021). Teacher Inquiry: Towards a typology of a teacher's inquiry disposition. *Professional Development in Education,* online. https://www.tandfonline.com/doi/full/10.1080/19415257.2021.187 9219?journalCode=rjie20

Dunn, R., Hattie, J., & Bowles, T. (2019). Exploring the experiences of teachers undertaking Educational Design Research (EDR) as a form of teacher professional learning. *Professional Development in Education, 45*(1), 151–167.

Dunst, C. J., & Hamby, D. W. (2015). A case study approach to secondary reanalysis of a quantitative research synthesis of adult learning practices studies. *International Journal of Learning, Teaching and Educational Research*, 13(3), 181–191.

Earl, L., & Timperley, H. (2015). Evaluative thinking for successful educational innovation. *OECD Education Working Papers*, No. 122. OECD Publishing. https://doi.org/10.1787/5jrxtk1jtdwf-en

Edelson, D. C. (2006). Balancing innovation and risk: Assessing design research proposals. In J. van den Akker, K. Gravemeijer, S. McKenney, & N. Nieveen (Eds.), *Education design research* (pp. 100–106). Routledge.

Edmondson, A. (1999). Psychological safety and learning behavior in work teams. *Administrative Science Quarterly*, 44(2), 350–383.

Edmondson, A. C. (2012). *Teaming: How organizations learn, innovate, and compete in the knowledge economy*. John Wiley & Sons.

Education Endowment Foundation. (2020). *EEF – Education Endowment Foundation*. https://educationendowmentfoundation.org.uk

Evidence for Learning. (2017). *The teaching and learning toolkit*. https://evidenceforlearning.org.au/the-toolkits/the-teaching-and-learning-toolkit/

Fisher, D., & Frey, N. (2014). Using teacher learning walks to improve instruction. *Principal Leadership*, 14(5), 58–61.

Fisher, D. B., Hattie, J., & Frey, N. (2016). *Visible learning for literacy, grades K-12: Implementing the practices that work best to accelerate student learning*. Corwin.

Fullan, M. (2011). *Change leader: Learning to do what matters most*. Jossey-Bass.

Fullan, M., & Hargreaves, A. (1996). *What's worth fighting for in your school?* (Rev. ed.). Teachers College Press.

Glickman, C., Gordon, S., & Ross-Gordon, J. M. (2004). Adult and teacher development within the context of the school: Clues for supervisory practice. In *Supervision and instructional leadership: A developmental approach* (6th ed., pp. 60–98). Allyn and Bacon.

Goodson, I. (1997). "Trendy theory" and teacher professionalism. *Cambridge Journal of Education*, 27(1), 7–22.

Gopalakrishnan, S, Preskill, H., & Lu, S. (2013). *Next generation evaluation: Embracing complexity, connectivity, and change*. Stanford Social Innovation Review. http://www.ssireview.org/nextgenevaluation

Green, K. L. (2011). *Complex adaptive systems in military analysis*. Institute for Defense Analyses. https://www.ida.org/-/media/feature/publications/c/co/complex-adaptive-systems-in-military-analysis/ida-document-d-4313.ashx

Grisogono, A. M., & Radenovic, V. (2007). The adaptive stance. *Complex*, 7, 2–5.

Grisogono, A. M., & Radenovic, V. (2011, June 26–July 1). *The Adaptive Stance – Steps towards teaching more effective complex decision-making*. Eighth International Conference on Complex Systems,

Quincy, MA, United States. https://www.researchgate.net/publication/275342327_The_Adaptive_Stance_-_steps_towards_teaching_more_effective_complex_decision-making

Guskey, T. R. (2002). Professional development and teacher change. *Teachers and Teaching: Theory and Practice, 8*(3), 381–391.

Hargreaves, A. (1994). *Changing teachers, changing times: Teachers' work and culture in the postmodern age.* OISE Press.

Hargreaves, A., & Fullan, M. (2012). *Professional capital: Transforming teaching in every school.* Teachers College Press.

Hattie, J. (2003). *Teachers make a difference – What is the research evidence?* Australian Council for Educational Research.

Hattie, J. A. C. (2009). *Visible learning: A synthesis of 800+ meta-analyses on achievement.* Routledge.

Hattie, J. (2015). High-impact leadership. *Educational Leadership, 72*(5), 36–40.

Hattie, J. A. C., & Clinton, J. M. (2011). School leaders as evaluators. In *Activate: A leader's guide to people, practices and processes* (pp. 93–118). The Leadership and Learning Center.

Hattie, J., & Smith, R. (Eds.). (2020). *10 Mindframes for leaders: The VISIBLE LEARNING (R) approach to school success.* Corwin.

Heifetz, R., Grashow, A., & Linsky, M. (2009). *The practice of adaptive leadership: Tools and tactics for changing your organization and the world.* Harvard Business Press.

Heifetz, R. A., & Laurie, D. L. (1997). The work of leadership. *Harvard Business Review, 75,* 124–134.

Hill, C. L., & Ridley, C. R. (2001). Diagnostic decision making: Do counselors delay final judgments? *Journal of Counseling & Development, 79(1),* 98–104.

Holyoak, K. J. (1991). Symbolic connectionism: Toward third-generation theories of expertise. In K. A. Ericsson & J. Smith (Eds.), *Toward a general theory of expertise: Prospects and limits* (pp. 301–335). Cambridge University Press.

Hopkins, D., & Craig, W. (2015). *Curiosity and powerful learning.* McREL Australia.

Hopkins, D., Munro, J., & Craig, W. (Eds.). (2011). *Powerful learning: A strategy for systemic educational improvement.* Australian Council for Educational Research.

Joyce, B., & Showers, B. (1994). Staff development and change process: Cut from the same cloth. *Issues . . . About Change, 4*(2). https://sedl.org/change/issues/issues42.html

Joyce, B., & Showers, B. (1995). Learning experiences in staff development. *The Developer, 3,* 523–554.

Joyce, B. R., & Showers, B. (2002). *Student achievement through staff development.* Association for Supervision and Curriculum Development.

https://www.unrwa.org/sites/default/files/joyce_and_showers_coaching_as_cpd.pdf

Karau, S. J., & Williams, K. D. (1993). Social loafing: A meta-analytic review and theoretical integration. *Journal of Personality and Social Psychology, 65*(4), 681–706.

Katz, D., & Kahn, R. L. (1978). *The social psychology of organizations* (2nd ed). Wiley.

Kirschner, P. A., & Surma, T. (2020, September 30). Evidence informed pedagogy. *Paul's Random Thoughts/Gedachten.* https://randomthought sandideas926468149.wordpress.com/2020/09/22/evidence-informed-pedagogy

Knight, J. (2012). *High-impact instruction: A framework for great teaching.* Corwin.

Kozlowski, S. W. J., Gully, S. M., Nason, E. R., & Smith, E. M. (1999). Developing adaptive teams: A theory of compilation and performance across levels and time. In D. R. Ilgen & E. D. Pulakos (Eds.), *The changing nature of work performance: Implications for staffing, personnel actions, and development* (pp. 240–292). Jossey-Bass.

Lee, J. C. K., & Day, C. (2016). Western and Chinese perspectives on quality and change in teacher education. In J. C. K. Lee & C. Day (Eds.), *Quality and change in teacher education: Western and Chinese perspectives* (pp. 1–16). Springer.

Loucks-Horsley, S., Hewson, P. W., Love, N., & Stiles, K. E. (1998). *Designing professional development for teachers of science and mathematics.* Corwin.

Loucks-Horsley, S., & Matsumoto, C. (1999). Research on professional development for teachers of mathematics and science: The state of the scene. *School Science and Mathematics, 99*(5), 258–271.

Lucas, B., Hanson, J., & Claxton, G. (2013). *Thinking like an engineer: Implications for the education system.* Royal Academy of Engineering.

Lucas, B., & Nacer, H. (2015). *The habits of an improver.* Health Foundation.

Maaranen, K. (2009). Practitioner research as part of professional development in initial teacher education. *Teacher Development, 13*(3), 219–237.

Marks, M. A., Zaccaro, S. J., & Mathieu, J. E. (2000). Performance implications of leader briefings and team-interaction training for team adaptation to novel environments. *Journal of Applied Psychology, 85*(6), 971–986.

Marzano, R. J. (2003). *What works in schools: Translating research into action.* ASCD.

McComb, S., & Simpson, V. (2014). The concept of shared mental models in healthcare collaboration. *Journal of Advanced Nursing, 70*(7), 1479–1488.

Menaker, E., MacDonald, J., Hendrick, A., & O'Connor, D. (2006). Training a Joint and Expeditionary Mindset. *ARI Contractor Report* 2007-04 (United States Army Research Institute for the Behavioral and Social Sciences), iii. https://www.researchgate.net/publication/235105649_Training_a_Joint_and_Expeditionary_Mindset/link/00b7d52b4a41432e86000000/download

Miller, E. (1995). The old model of staff development survives in a world where everything else has changed. *The Harvard Education Letter, XI*(1).

Miller, J. H., & Page, S. E. (2007). *Complex adaptive systems: An introduction to computational models of social life.* Princeton University Press.

Mohammed, S., Klimoski, R., & Rentsch, J. R. (2000). The measurement of team mental models: We have no shared schema. *Organizational Research Methods, 3*(2), 123–165. https://doi.org/10.1177/109442810032001

Mourshed, M., Chijioke, C., & Barber, M. (2010). *How the world's most improved school systems keep getting better.* McKinsey.

NSW Department of Education. (2015). *Effective leadership.* Centre for Education Statistics and Evaluation. https://www.cese.nsw.gov.au//images/stories/PDF/EffectiveLeadership_%20Learning_Curve_10_AA.pdf

Nutley, S. M., Walter, I., & Davies, H. T. O. (2007). *Using evidence: How research can inform public services.* Policy Press.

Opfer, V. D., & Pedder, D. (2011). Conceptualizing teacher professional learning. *Review of Educational Research, 81*(3), 376–407.

Orland-Barak, L. (2006). Convergent, divergent and parallel dialogues: Knowledge construction in professional conversations. *Teachers and Teaching: Theory and Practice, 12*(1), 13–31.

Pearsall, M. J., Ellis, A. P. J., & Bell, B. S. (2010). *Building the infrastructure: The effects of role identification behaviors on team cognition development and performance.* https://core.ac.uk/download/pdf/144981727.pdf

Perkins, D. N., Jay, E., & Tishman, S. (1993). Beyond abilities: A dispositional theory of thinking. *Merrill-Palmer Quarterly: Journal of Developmental Psychology, 39*(1), 1–21.

Plomp, T. (2007). *Education design research: An introduction.* In T. Plomp & N. Nieveen (Eds.), *An introduction to educational design research* (pp. 9–35). Netherlands Institute for Curriculum Development.

Reeves, D. B. (2012). *Transforming professional development into student results.* ASCD.

Re:Work with Google. (n.d.). Identify dynamics of effective teams. In *Guide: Understand team effectiveness.* https://rework.withgoogle.com/guides/understanding-team-effectiveness/steps/identify-dynamics-of-effective-teams

Rickards, Hattie, & Reid. (2021). www.taylorfrancis.com/books/turning-point-teaching-profession-field-rickards-john-hattie-catherine-reid/ 10.4324/9781003080831

Robinson, V. M. (2010). From instructional leadership to leadership capabilities: Empirical findings and methodological challenges. *Leadership and Policy in Schools, 9*(1), 1–26.

Robinson, V. (2017). *Reduce change to increase improvement* [Corwin Impact Leadership series]. Corwin.

Rosenshine, B. (2010). *Principles of instruction.* International Academy of Education.

Rouse, W. B., Cannon-Bowers, J. A., & Salas, E. (1992). The role of mental models in team performance in complex systems. *IEEE Transactions on Systems, Man, & Cybernetics, 22*(6), 1296–1308. https://doi.org/ 10.1109/21.199457

Rouse, W. B., & Morris, N. M. (1986). On looking into the black box: Prospects and limits in the search for mental models. *Psychological Bulletin, 100*(3), 349–363. https://doi.org/10.1037/0033-2909.100.3.349

Rubie-Davies, C. (2014). *Becoming a high expectation teacher: Raising the bar.* Routledge.

Schön, D. (1983). *The reflective practitioner: How professionals think in action.* Basic Books.

Schön, D. A. (1987). *Educating the reflective practitioner: Toward a new design for teaching and learning in the professions.* Jossey-Bass.

Schwandt, T. A. (2008). Educating for intelligent belief in evaluation. *American Journal of Evaluation, 29*(2), 139–150.

Servage, L. (2008, Winter). Critical and transformative practices in professional learning communities. *Teacher Education Quarterly,* 63–77.

Sharples, J. (2013, June). *Evidence for the frontline: A report for the Alliance for Useful Evidence.* Alliance for Useful Evidence. https://www.allian ce4usefulevidence.org/assets/EVIDENCE-FOR-THE-FRONTLINE-FINAL-5-June-2013.pdf

Shepherd, J. P. (2007). The production and management of evidence for public service reform. *Evidence and Policy, 3*(2), 231–251.

Sims, S., & Fletcher-Wood, H. (2020). Identifying the characteristics of effective teacher professional development: A critical review. *School Effectiveness and School Improvement,* 1–17. doi:10.1080/0924345 3.2020.1772841

Sparks, D. (2004). The looming danger of a two-tiered professional development system. *Phi Delta Kappan, 86*(4), 304–308.

Supovitz, J. A. (2001). Translating teaching practice into improved student achievement. In S. Fuhrman (Ed.), *From the Capitol to the classroom: Standards-based reforms in the States* [The one hundredth yearbook of the National Society for the Study of Education] (Part 2, pp. 81–98). University of Chicago Press.

Symons, D., & Dunn, R. (2019). Productive discussion as a foundation for primary mathematics. *Australian Primary Mathematics Classroom,* *24*(2), 21–25. https://www.researchgate.net/publication/334696231_Productive_discussion_as_a_foundation_for_primary_mathematics

Timperley, H. (2015). *Professional conversations and improvement-focused feedback: A review of the research literature and the impact on practice and student outcomes.* Australian Institute for Teaching and School Leadership. https://www.aitsl.edu.au/docs/default-source/default-document-library/professional-conversations-literature-review-oct-2015.pdf

Timperley, H., Wilson, A., Barrar, H., & Fung, I. (2007). *Teacher professional learning and development: Best evidence synthesis iteration.* New Zealand Ministry of Education.

Veenman, M. V. J. (2008). Giftedness: Predicting the speed of expertise acquisition by intellectual ability and metacognitive skillfulness of novices. In M. F. Shaughnessy, M. V. J. Veenman, & C. K. Kennedy (Eds.), *Meta-cognition: A recent review of research, theory, and perspectives* (pp. 207–220). Nova Science Publishers.

Von Stumm, S., Hell, B., & Chamorro-Premuzic, T. (2011). The hungry mind: Intellectual curiosity is the third pillar of academic performance. *Perspectives on Psychological Science, 6*(6), 574–588.

Walter, C., & Briggs, J. (2012). *What professional development makes the most difference to teachers? A report sponsored by Oxford University Press.* https://www.researchgate.net/publication/261989819_What_professional_development_makes_the_most_difference_to_teachers_A_report_sponsored_by_Oxford_University_Press

Wei, R. C., Darling-Hammond, L., Andree, A., Richardson, N., & Orphanos, S. (2009). *Professional learning in the learning profession: A status report on teacher development in the United States and abroad.* National Staff Development Council.

Willingham, D. (2014). Making students more CURIOUS. *Knowledge Quest, 42*(5), 32–35.

Yoon, K. S., Duncan, T., Lee, S. W.-Y., Scarloss, B., & Shapley, K. (2007). *Reviewing the evidence on how teacher professional development affects student achievement* (Issues & Answers Report, REL 2007–No. 033). US Department of Education, Institute of Education Sciences, National Center for Education Evaluation and Regional Assistance, Regional Educational Laboratory Southwest. https://www.researchgate.net/publication/234730012_Reviewing_the_Evidence_on_How_Teacher_Professional_Development_Affects_Student_Achievement_Issues_Answers_REL_2007-No_033/link/0fcfd511e53699fdf5000000/download

Index

A SAGE Publishing Company

Helping educators make the greatest impact

CORWIN HAS ONE MISSION: to enhance education through intentional professional learning.

We build long-term relationships with our authors, educators, clients, and associations who partner with us to develop and continuously improve the best evidence-based practices that establish and support lifelong learning.

Leadership That Makes an Impact

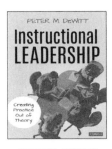

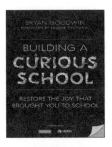

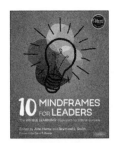

**MICHAEL FULLAN &
MARY JEAN GALLAGHER**

With the goal of transforming the culture of learning to develop greater equity, excellence, and student well-being, this book will help you liberate the system and maintain focus.

PETER M. DEWITT

This step-by-step how-to guide presents the six driving forces of instructional leadership within a multistage model for implementation, delivering lasting improvement through small collaborative changes.

BRYAN GOODWIN

If you've ever wondered anything, really—just out of curiosity—then you have what it takes to lead your school to restored curiosity and your students to well-being and success.

**JOHN HATTIE &
RAYMOND L. SMITH**

Based on the most current Visible Learning® research with contributions from education thought leaders around the world, this book includes practical ideas for leaders to implement high-impact strategies to strengthen entire school cultures and advocate for all students.

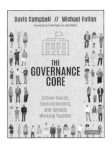

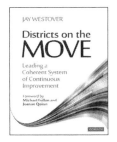

**DAVIS CAMPBELL &
MICHAEL FULLAN**

The model outlined in this book develops a systems approach to governing local schools collaboratively to become exemplars of highly effective decision-making, leadership, and action.

**MICHAEL FULLAN,
JOANNE QUINN, &
JOANNE MCEACHEN**

The comprehensive strategy of deep learning incorporates practical tools and processes to engage educational stakeholders in new partnerships, mobilize whole-system change, and transform learning for all students.

**JOANNE QUINN,
JOANNE MCEACHEN,
MICHAEL FULLAN,
MAG GARDNER, &
MAX DRUMMY**

Dive into deep learning with this hands-on guide to creating learning experiences that give purpose, unleash student potential, and transform not only learning, but life itself.

JAY WESTOVER

The transformative framework outlined in this book creates a districtwide approach for changing the culture of learning and creating a coherent system of continuous improvement.

ANTHONY KIM, KEARA MASCARENAZ, & KAWAI LAI

This guide provides battle-tested practices to help leaders build better habits for team learning, meetings, and projects, to achieve a more responsive, innovative organization.

EVAN ROBB

Build the foundations of effective leadership despite daily distractions. Learn how to intentionally use ten-minute opportunities to consider and execute your vision.

AMY TEPPER & PATRICK FLYNN

Nineteen strategies help leaders, coaches, and teachers improve their ability to identify desired outcomes, recognize learning in action, collect relevant evidence, and develop effective feedback.

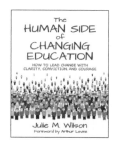

JULIE M. WILSON

Learn to make sense of challenging change journeys and accelerate implementation with this practical framework that includes human-centered tools, resources, and mini case studies.

GRANT LICHTMAN

Our rapidly evolving world is dramatically impacting how we view schools. *Thrive* shows educators how they can help their schools not only survive but thrive during rapid change.

ERIC SHENINGER

The future-forward framework in this book prepares leaders to harness the power of innovative ideas and digital strategies to create relevant, engaging, and intuitive school cultures.

CHRISTINE MASON, PAUL LIABENOW, & MELISSA PATSCHKE

Envision and enact transformative change with an iterative visioning process, thought-provoking vignettes, case studies from exemplary schools, key strategies and tools, and practical implementation ideas.

KIRSTEN RICHERT, JEFFREY IKLER, & MARGARET ZACCHEI

Shifting empowers educational change leaders to proactively and coherently navigate complex, unprecedented change in schools and establish a school culture in which changemakers can thrive.